Jeanette Winterson and Religion

NEW DIRECTIONS IN RELIGION AND LITERATURE

This series aims to showcase new work at the forefront of religion and literature through short studies written by leading and rising scholars in the field. Books will pursue a variety of theoretical approaches as they engage with writing from different religious and literary traditions. Collectively, the series will offer a timely critical intervention to the interdisciplinary crossover between religion and literature, speaking to wider contemporary interests and mapping out new directions for the field in the early twenty-first century.

Series editors: Emma Mason and Mark Knight

ALSO AVAILABLE IN THE SERIES:

The New Atheist Novel, Arthur Bradley and Andrew Tate
Blake. Wordsworth. Religion, Jonathan Roberts
Do the Gods Wear Capes?, Ben Saunders
England's Secular Scripture, Jo Carruthers
Victorian Parables, Susan E. Colón
The Late Walter Benjamin, John Schad
Dante and the Sense of Transgression, William Franke
The Glyph and the Gramophone, Luke Ferretter
John Cage and Buddhist Ecopoetics, Peter Jaeger
Rewriting the Old Testament in Anglo-Saxon Verse, Samantha Zacher
Forgiveness in Victorian Literature, Richard Hughes Gibson
The Gospel According to the Novelist, Magdalena Mączyńska
Jewish Feeling, Richa Dwor
Beyond the Willing Suspension of Disbelief, Michael Tomko

The Gospel According to David Foster Wallace, Adam S. Miller
Pentecostal Modernism, Stephen Shapiro and Philip Barnard
The Bible in the American Short Story, Lesleigh Cushing Stahlberg and Peter S. Hawkins
Faith in Poetry, Michael D. Hurley

FORTHCOMING:

Religion and American Literature Since 1950, Mark Eaton
Romantic Enchantment, Gavin Hopps
Esoteric Islam in Modern French Thought, Ziad Elmarsafy
Marilynne Robinson's Worldly Gospel, Ryan S. Kemp and Jordan M. Rodgers
Weird Faith in 19th Century Literature, Mark Knight and Emma Mason

Jeanette Winterson and Religion

Emily McAvan

BLOOMSBURY ACADEMIC
LONDON • NEW YORK • OXFORD • NEW DELHI • SYDNEY

BLOOMSBURY ACADEMIC
Bloomsbury Publishing Plc
50 Bedford Square, London, WC1B 3DP, UK
1385 Broadway, New York, NY 10018, USA
29 Earlsfort Terrace, Dublin 2, Ireland

BLOOMSBURY, BLOOMSBURY ACADEMIC and the Diana logo
are trademarks of Bloomsbury Publishing Plc

First published in Great Britain 2020
This paperback edition published in 2021

Copyright © Emily McAvan, 2020

Emily McAvan has asserted her right under the Copyright, Designs and Patents Act, 1988, to be identified as Author of this work.

Cover design: Eleanor Rose
Cover photograph © Getty Images

All rights reserved. No part of this publication may be reproduced or transmitted in any form or by any means, electronic or mechanical, including photocopying, recording, or any information storage or retrieval system, without prior permission in writing from the publishers.

Bloomsbury Publishing Plc does not have any control over, or responsibility for, any third-party websites referred to or in this book. All internet addresses given in this book were correct at the time of going to press. The author and publisher regret any inconvenience caused if addresses have changed or sites have ceased to exist, but can accept no responsibility for any such changes.

The third party copyrighted material displayed in the pages of this book are done so on the basis of fair dealing for the purposes of criticism, review, teaching, scholarship or research only in accordance with international copyright laws, and is not intended to infringe upon the ownership rights of the original owners.

A catalogue record for this book is available from the British Library.

Library of Congress Control Number: 2019949578

ISBN: HB: 978-1-3500-9690-5
PB: 978-1-3502-3595-3
ePDF: 978-1-3500-9691-2
eBook: 978-1-3500-9692-9

Series: New Directions in Religion and Literature

Typeset by Integra Software Services Pvt Ltd.

To find out more about our authors and books visit www.bloomsbury.com and sign up for our newsletters.

This book is dedicated to my wife Elizabeth and my daughter Amelia, for everything.

Thank you to Tom Cho, Jessica Durham and Jenny Lee, and all the friends with whom I've talked books.

Contents

Introduction   1

1. 'I Love Both of Them': Queer Love and the Religious in *Oranges Are Not the Only Fruit*   17
2. 'Colours and Folly': Retelling the Noah Story in *Boating for Beginners*   31
3. The Love Event in *The Passion*   45
4. *Sexing the Cherry* and the Monstrous Maternal   61
5. *Written on the Body* and the Negative Theology Tradition   75
6. *Art & Lies*: Literature in a Neoliberal Age   87
7. *Gut Symmetries*, New Physics and Kabbalah   103
8. *The PowerBook* and Virtual Culture   119
9. *Lighthousekeeping* and the Religious Vocation   133
10. Climate Change Apocalypse and *The Stone Gods*   149

Conclusion   163

Notes   171
Bibliography   201
Index   210

Introduction

Contemporary British novelist Jeanette Winterson is one of the most important writers currently working in the English language. Although her corpus has been much discussed by critics, these academic discussions have primarily centred on gender, sexuality and postmodernism. Feminist critics have drawn our attention to the ways in which Winterson's writing imagines female-centred relationships, culture and language, while queer critics have noted the fluidity of representations of gender and sexuality in Winterson's books. Winterson's relation to lesbian feminism and her gender essentialism (or lack thereof) have been hotly debated topics. Postmodern critics, on the other hand, have revelled in Winterson's playful use of language and her flair with reworking history, language and myth into new, creative formulations.

But while gender and sexuality are undoubtedly an important part of Winterson's corpus, this critical focus leaves out a vital force in Winterson's writing: religion. Since the beginnings of her career in the autobiographical *Oranges Are Not the Only Fruit*, Jeanette Winterson's novels have entangled religion with gender and sexuality, particularly queer sexuality. There are varying imaginings of gender and sexuality that have captured the imagination of critics, from the 'gender undeclared' narrator of *Written on the Body* to the bisexual love triangles in *The Passion*, *Gut Symmetries* and *The PowerBook*. At the same time, not only has Winterson rewritten stories from the Bible – e.g. the Noah retelling of *Boating for Beginners* and the Nativity retelling in her children's book *The Lion, the Unicorn and Me* – but also many of the characters are religious in some sense, ranging from priests (Patrick in *The Passion*, Handel in *Art & Lies*), reverends (Babel Dark in *Lighthousekeeping*), fundamentalists (Louie in *Oranges*), Jews (Elgin in *Written on the Body* and Stella and her father in *Gut Symmetries*) to run-of-the-mill Christian believers (Henri in *The Passion* and Elsie in *Oranges*). As a result, I argue that Winterson's work cannot be fully understood divorced of a knowledge of the religious, primarily Christian, thread that runs right through her body of work. Drawing heavily on Christian (and occasionally Jewish) themes and motifs, Winterson's books collapse the boundaries of sacred and profane by grounding her studies of sexuality and gender play in a tradition of religious imagery. In this book, I will suggest that Winterson expresses the sacred through the bodily, that her novels tarry with various forms of 'otherness', and that Winterson's work collapses the boundaries between the transcendent and the immanent, the secular and the religious. Rather than simply discarding the gendered, sexual and linguistic preoccupations of earlier critics, I will draw on this body of work and supplement it with a persistent focus on the sacred as it emerges in Winterson's writing.

In doing so, I will bring this important writer into conversation with contemporary feminist and queer theologians like Catherine Keller and Marcella Althaus-Reid, as well as the 'theological turn' of notable theorists like Alain Badiou, Jacques Derrida, John Caputo, Richard Kearney, Julia Kristeva and Luce Irigaray. I am interested in reading Winterson next to and against these writers, showing Winterson's work as having strong resonances with post-structuralist philosophy and theology, as well as a distinctive quality all of its own. This theoretical framework will allow the reader to understand the critical stakes in Winterson's work, as well as the broader theological and philosophical background at work in writing literature after the death of God. The death of God, which was declared by Nietzsche and taken up again after the Second World War by Christian and Jewish theologians, profoundly influences the ways in which contemporary formulations of the religious are formed. I argue that Winterson's work is best understood as a form of what Mark Taylor calls in his book *Erring* an 'a/ theology', an approach to the sacred in which there is a deconstructive hesitation.[1] Writing in the mid-1980s, but in words still relevant today, Taylor talks about 'marginal people [who] constantly live on the border that both joins and separates belief and unbelief. They look yet do not find, search but do not discover. This failure, however, need not necessarily end the quest.'[2] It is my contention that Winterson's work is one of the literary sites in contemporary culture where we may find attention given to the borders between belief and unbelief that Taylor describes, and it is for this reason an important one. Where so many of the religious debates in the world are shaped by competing forms of fundamentalism, Winterson's writing provides a provocative, questioning approach to the sacred, accepting none of the platitudes of religious belief but acknowledging the power and comfort of religious practice in ways that trouble any easy categorization of Winterson as an atheist writer either. *The Passion*'s Villanelle, for instance, is 'never tempted by God but [she] likes his trappings', attending services at 'churches because they were built from the heart'.[3] Religious practice is just one of the forms of passion in the novel, one of the stories people tell, with its playful catch-cry blurring of the boundaries between fiction and truth – 'I'm telling you stories. Trust me.'[4]

So, although numerous writers have implicitly considered Winterson from a strictly secular perspective, I instead will take a post-secular approach, in which it is the very aesthetics of literature that create the conditions for an experience of the sacred – not the kind one might find in a church or synagogue, but a more complicated one on the page. In his mid-century collection *Theology of Culture*, Paul Tillich questions the apparent secularism of art, suggesting that art answers 'the ultimate meaning of life'. He states that: 'Whatever the subject matter which an artist chooses, however strong or weak his [*sic*] artistic form, he cannot but help betray by his style his own ultimate concern, as well as that of his group, and his period. He cannot escape religion even if he rejects religion, for religion is the state of being ultimately concerned.'[5] Tillich's argument therefore suggests that the opposition between secular and religious in culture is a problematic one, and that through style art raises questions that are ultimately religious. Although Tillich was more of an existentialist than post-structuralist, I am interested in his work for its ability to question the either/or nature of debate around the religious and its relation to culture. As Taylor has put it, 'religion is most interesting where it is least obvious'.[6] Primarily received as a lesbian and a feminist, Jeanette Winterson has not generally been considered a religious thinker, and yet it is the religious thread running through her work that is one of the most intriguing aspects of her as a writer. It is precisely in her style, as Tillich suggests, that Winterson betrays her interest in the divine. I argue that it is through literature that contemporary subjects might experience a kind of religious encounter. This might appear to create few ethical or material demands in terms of dogma or community service – which is extremely important when we consider Winterson's experiences with Christianity as a lesbian – but, as my analysis of Winterson's texts will show, ethical responsibility is never far from the frame. So, although Winterson's writing does not require regular church-going or a belief in a rigid canon of theological thought, her novels demand an embrace of passion on the part of their readers, a reinvention of the circumstances of one's life in response to an encounter with otherness. To borrow a phrase from Richard Kearney, Winterson writes religion as art, and art as religion.[7]

Winterson's postmodern language

Culture has long sought to displace religion as a (*the*, even) source of meaning and transcendence, for, as Terry Eagleton notes, 'most aesthetic ideas (creation, inspiration, unity, autonomy, symbol, epiphany and so on) are really displaced fragments of theology.'[8] Or as Winterson puts it in *Art Objects*: 'I grew up not knowing that language was for everyday purposes. I grew up with the Word and the Word was God. Now, many years after a secular Reformation, I still think of language as something holy.'[9] Winterson may not believe in God – or, at the very least, not an interventionist God – but her writing is distinctive for the ways in which it treats language as *sacramental*, set apart, a fragment of the divine. While Winterson's work does not evince belief of a transcendent God, it does show evidence for seeing the sacred *in* the profane world of language, materiality and embodiment. Her interest in the other, indeed in otherness itself, transmutes the body of the beloved into something sacred. Winterson's negation of the transcendental God then is not strictly an atheist manoeuvre, for 'negation [...] is not necessarily denial'[10] when it comes to the religious. The post-secular negates both belief and unbelief in its moving beyond those easy binaries. Arguably, Winterson's work moves into the cultural space after secularism, the long tail after the death of God.

It is therefore through a heightened attention to language that Winterson approaches the sacred. In *Why Be Happy When You Could Be Normal?*, Winterson argues that we need to replace institutionalized religion with secularized forms that speak to us. She argues that 'the Western world has done away with religion but not with our religious impulses; we seem to need some higher purpose, some point to our lives – money and leisure, social progress, are just not enough. We shall have to find new ways of finding meaning – it is not yet clear how this will happen.'[11] And in *Art Objects*:

> Art is visionary; it sees beyond the view from the window, even though the window is its frame. This is why the arts fare much better alongside religion than alongside either capitalism or communism. The god-instinct and the art-instinct both apprehend more than the physical biological world. The artist need not believe in God, but the artist does consider reality as multiple and complex.[12]

Winterson clearly sees an affinity between her work as a writer and the impulses that motivate religious practice and thought. In treating art as religion, Winterson elevates the profane into the sacred. Indeed, art has come to occupy a sacred place in Winterson's writing, for as she explains in an interview with Eleanor Wachtel, art is a 'sanctified space […] there is something cathedral-like about it: it's a place where you can rest, contemplate, refuel and go out again knowing that it remains there for you'.[13] This quasi-religious function of art is something that Winterson returns to over and over again in her work, especially in *Art & Lies*, a novel as polemical in its own way as Winterson's collection of essays *Art Objects*.

Of course, numerous critics have lauded Winterson's use of language over the course of her career. In particular, postmodern critics from the early 1990s onwards have praised the ways in which Winterson's writing shows a linguistic fluidity. In the collection *The Lesbian Postmodern*, Laura Doan has influentially argued that 'what [Judith] Butler pioneers theoretically, Winterson enacts in her metafictional writing practices: a sexual politics of heterogeniety and a vision of hybridized gender constructions outside an either/or proposition, at once political and postmodern'.[14] Doan accurately notes the way in which Winterson plays with gender, from the 'gender undeclared' narrator of *Written on the Body* to the cross-dressing in *Sexing the Cherry* and *The Passion*. Indeed, feminist critics have long noted Winterson's collapsing of gender and sexual boundaries in the gender experimentation and bisexuality themes of her work of the 1980s and 1990s. Moreover, the metafictional conceits in Winterson's early work – as seen in *The Passion*'s emblematic tag line, 'I'm telling you stories. Trust me' – problematize popular realist concepts of stories as mimetic, instead paying a characteristically postmodern attention to the linguistically constructed qualities of history, self, gender and sexuality. So, where modern texts create binary oppositions, critics like Doan see Winterson as deconstructing binaries in a postmodern fashion, blurring the lines between apparent opposites. Further, the experimental nature of *Oranges Are Not the Only Fruit*, with its protagonist Jeanette, blurs the lines between autobiography and fiction, history and narrative, real and unreal.

Yet this postmodern critical interest in Winterson's language has left out its clear deconstruction of the religious/secular binary. The narrator of *Written on the Body* warns: 'it's the clichés that cause the problems'[15] – and not just the gendered and sexual clichés, but the religious ones too. Where Jeanette's fundamentalist mother Louie in *Oranges* has a list of 'enemies' and 'friends', the text itself has a more complicated view of attachments, questioning easy oppositions, including the religion that harms Jeanette through its homophobia. Arguably, Winterson's problematizing of the boundary between religious and secular is one of the most significant – and powerful – elements in her work, yet it has been strangely overlooked by literary critics and theorists. While Winterson undoubtedly uses the Bible as the 'Great Code' (I take this phrase from Northrop Frye, who borrowed it from William Blake)[16] for her writing, perhaps most modern criticism itself operates in a more secular vein. And yet we must account for the strong current of religious imagery in Winterson's work in a sustained and compelling way, for it situates Winterson as one of the foremost writers of the twentieth and twenty-first centuries grappling with the death of God.

So, what does it mean to think of Winterson as a writer whose work comes after the death of God? It means first and foremost the absence of an interventionist God. This is no great innovation on its own, for many modern writers write worlds without God – it is basic secularism. The historical events of the twentieth century – not to mention the modernity of the nineteenth that Nietzsche was responding to – have put paid to that model of God. Winterson moves beyond the simply secular into a more complicated post-secularism, in which the forms of religious practice still remain as powerful sources of experience, and where there is a clear sense of the transcendent in the immanent. I argue that Winterson's work engages with philosophical ideas (especially those promulgated by post-structuralist and deconstructive theorists and theologians) that have emerged after the death of God in her engagement with otherness, which has gendered and sexual implications as well as theological. But deconstructive texts – and numerous critics have argued powerfully that at least some of Winterson's work is deconstructive – also may be seen as the *poetics* of the death of God, with the postmodern scrambling of hierarchies including the religion/secular one comprising a key feature of literature after the Second World War. As Kearney has said: 'If poetics invites a "willing suspension" of first belief and disbelief, it neither includes or excludes a leap of second faith [but it] may be said to clear a landing site for the divine stranger.'[17]

The otherness of post-secular literature

In her collapsing of the religious/secular binary, Winterson scrambles one more divide – that between human and divine. This is a move that has some parallels in post-structuralist theory and theology. In *The Gift of Death*, Jacques Derrida argues that the infinite alterity of God differs little in the end from the infinite alterity of any other other. '*Tout autre est tout autre*', as he puts it in French. Derrida underlines the otherness of the human, stating that 'everyone else […] is infinitely other in its absolute singularity, inaccessibility, solitary, transcendent'.[18] Therefore, 'what can be said about Abraham's relation to God [in Genesis][19] can be said about my relation without relation to every one (one) as every (bit) other'.[20] Derrida's position thus can be seen to underline the divinity of relationships between people, and the opacity of the other – any other – prevents us from making any hard distinctions between God and other.

It is this deconstructive hesitation between God and other, introduced in the literary work – and specifically Winterson's work – that I wish to advance in this book, following on from the deconstructive theologians and philosophers of religion who have taken up Derrida's challenge to the onto-theological tradition of positive theology. Kearney, Taylor and Caputo have all made their contributions to the deconstructionist theology of the last several decades. Taylor argues for a form of religious reading that takes in the hesitation of the slash, that is neither atheistic nor theological (in its classical deist triumphalist incarnation) but is instead both and neither. A/theology, as Taylor explains it, is a critical manoeuvre that deconstructs the binaries that have defined both humanist atheism and onto-theology. In a famous phrase, he argues that 'deconstruction is the "hermeneutic" of the death of God'.[21] He writes for what he calls 'marginal' people, people who 'constantly live on the border that both joins and separates belief and unbelief. They look yet do not find, search but do not discover.'[22]

I wish to pursue Winterson's writing as a form of a/theology, a writing that lives on the border between sacred and profane, belief and unbelief. Rather than solely claiming Winterson for a religious project, I argue that her work functions in an a/theological fashion in the way that it approaches otherness. In short, I wish to argue that Winterson's work produces a deconstructive hesitation between self and other, others and God, using a wide range of religiously inflected voices that conjure an otherness that may, or may not, be considered religious in certain senses. In doing so, I will read Winterson in relation to post-structuralist (and beyond) thought about the sacred, the body and the word.

Winterson and the desiring/desired other

There is repeated attention given to the otherness of the other in Winterson's writing with profound a/theological connotations. In her review of *The PowerBook* in the *Guardian* newspaper, Elaine Showalter drew our attention to Winterson's 'eternal triangles', the 'adulterous bisexual love'[23] story that Winterson tells in a number of texts including *The Passion, Gut Symmetries, The PowerBook* and *Written on the Body* (depending on one's reading). But where Showalter sees 'literary junk food', I argue that the recurrence of the love triangle shows a beloved with split affections – the philosophical question 'what does the other want' becomes a very real problem for the protagonists of these texts. For the lover of a married woman (and it is always a married *woman* in Winterson) is one who cannot be sure of their position, made anxious by the beloved's divided loyalties. The beloved other cannot ever be fully known or understood.

To the casual reader, this interest in the other – and their body – may seem simply profane, bound up in this-worldly preoccupations with gender and sexuality (and certainly many critics of Winterson have read her in this way). Yet the work of Derrida and those who have followed him might suggest a more nuanced take on Winterson's writing. In *The Passion*, for instance, Henri reflects on the otherness of the beloved, an alterity that must be respected, cherished:

> I am in love with her; not a fantasy or a myth or a creature of my own making.
> Her. A person who is not me [...]
> My passion for her, even though she could never return it, showed me the difference between inventing a lover and falling in love.
> The one is about you, the other about someone else.[24]

Henri's love for Villanelle, as we shall discover in greater depth in Chapter 3, is about a serene kind of acceptance of the otherness of the beloved – in the end, Henri prefers to stay in the San Servolo prison rather than accept Villanelle's half-hearted sisterly love. The 'not me'-ness of the beloved other is precious in itself, even when unreturned. For Winterson, especially the early Winterson of the late

1980s and early 1990s, passion is the pre-eminent value, an embodied encounter that signals beyond the illusory nature of the narcissistic play of the self ('fantasy or a myth or a creature') to a real encounter with other. And yet the opacity of the other – which Derrida would suggest blurs the boundaries between the human and the divine – is irreducible and vital.

This interest in the other can be seen throughout Winterson's work. Literary critic Jennifer Gustar argues that Winterson's work 'evinces a commitment to revivify and transform language; and reveals evidence of an "other" language, one that expresses desire by keeping language in motion'.[25] Winterson's approach to the other is mediated by the distinctly sexual implications of language. As Sappho in *Art & Lies* puts it: 'the word and the kiss are one. Is language sex? Say my name and you say sex.'[26] In a startling passage, Sappho compares language to a strap-on dildo: 'This is the nature of our sex. She takes a word, straps it on, penetrates me hard. The word inside me, I become it. The word slots my belly, my belly swells the word. New meanings expand from my thighs. Together we have sacked the dictionary for a lexigraphic fuck.'[27]

What critic Christy Burns calls Winterson's 'liturgical style'[28] is a fully embodied language that takes in the whole of her characters, including gendered and sexual desires. Burns underlines the fantastic nature of language and desire in Winterson. But where feminist and queer critics have read Winterson as a secular writer experimenting with form, and thus new forms of gender and sexual identity and practice, we must also supplement this perspective with an a/theological impulse that sees the sacred in the bodily, in the materiality of the language that Winterson uses.

Winterson is at pains, especially in her early work, to radically rework the language of romance narratives, not only changing the gendered and sexual roles of the participants – many of her characters are lesbian or bisexual, after all, a far from usual feature of fiction –

but attempting to change the imagery of eroticism and feeling. For instance, the aquatic imagery of *Written on the Body* recalls Cixous' call for an *ecriture feminine*,[29] a writing of the female body: 'She smells of the sea. She smells of rockpools when I was a child. She keeps a starfish in there. I crouch down to taste the salt, to run my fingers around the rim. She opens and shuts like a sea anemone. She's refilled each day with fresh tides of longing.'[30]

Against the tired phallocentric imagery of traditional heterosexual romance narratives, Winterson constructs a female-centric queer language that encompasses a multiplicity of desiring positions – an extraordinarily original contribution to English literature that has been rarely attempted. So, far from participating in the postmodern exhaustion with language and narrative as seen in other contemporaneous writers like Don DeLillo, Winterson aims at a re-invention of narrative through an infusion of poetic language into contemporary literature. It is in this sense that Winterson may be seen as coming *after* postmodernism, of being post-postmodern (if one may use that awkward portmanteau).[31] Yet we may also see this 'other' language that Gustar describes at work in Winterson's writing as religious too. It is no coincidence that Winterson's writing attempts to revitalize narrative in part through religious language, at a time in which religion has returned in many multifarious forms after the death of God. Winterson's *ecriture feminine* is a fascinating invocation of an embodied sacred.

We may consider Winterson's interest in the alterity of the other, then, as a form of modern mysticism that experiences the transcendent through the immanent, the spiritual through the flesh. As Michel de Certeau put it in an article on mysticism, 'mysticism found its modern social language in the body'.[32] This has its parallels with some modern forms of phenomenology, for example, in the work of Maurice Merleau-Ponty. In his phenomenological approach to the material, Merleau-Ponty has a profoundly eucharistic approach:

> Just as the sacrament not only symbolizes, in sensible species, an operation of Grace, but *is* also the real presence of God, which it causes to occupy a fragment of space and communicates to those that eat of the consecrated bread, provided that they are inwardly prepared, in the same way the sensible has not only a motor but a vital significance, but is nothing other than a certain way of being in the world suggested to us from some point in space, and seized and acted upon by our body, provided that it is capable of doing so, so the sensation is literally a form of communion.[33]

For Merleau-Ponty, the sacrament is simultaneously material *and* symbolic. In *The Passion*, we also see the collapse of material and symbolic, with Villanelle's very real heart imprisoned in the house of the Queen of Spades. Winterson is ever aware of the material consequences of insubstantial words and actions.

We can therefore see the body of the other in Winterson as a form of phenomenological sacramentality, calling to the transcendent through the immanent. The hospitality to otherness described by Derrida becomes, in Winterson, a hospitality to fleshly contact with the other's body – a divine erotics of welcome. As she puts it in *Written on the Body*:

> 'Explore me', you said and I collected my ropes, flasks and maps, expecting to be back home soon. I dropped into the mass of you and I cannot find the way out. Sometimes I think I'm free, coughed up like Jonah from the whale, but then I turn a corner and recognise myself again. Myself in your skin, myself lodged in your bones, myself floating in the cavities that decorate every surgeon's wall. That is how I know you. You are what I know.[34]

Recalling the Biblical euphemism of 'knowing' as sexual knowledge, Winterson's narrator 'knows' her partner Louise intimately, both as a lover and through the anatomy textbooks she consults when Louise contracts cancer. Even apparent freedom from the other is imagined in Biblical terms ('coughed up like Jonah'), although that turns out to be a misrecognition of detachment from the beloved and therefore the self. The other is not so easily put aside.

The hospitality to the other even at times in Winterson becomes almost a kind of hostage taking, recalling a key image of Emmanuel Levinas.[35] In *The Passion*, for instance, she asks: 'Do all lovers feel helpless and valiant in the presence of the beloved? Helpless because the need to roll over like a pet dog is never far away. Valiant because you know you would slay a dragon with a pocket knife if you had to.'[36] Or as she muses in *Oranges Are Not the Only Fruit*, 'on the wild nights who can you call home? Only the one who knows your name.'[37] The other exerts a kind of thrall over the Wintersonian lover, with a bifurcated edge. For Derrida, one can never know ahead of time if the other will be hostile or hospitable,[38] and this is equally true for Winterson. And yet it is clear from these very modern romances that this is the risk of every relationship and, in particular, with the corporeal vulnerability of loving.

In doing so, Winterson's work provides an even more profound religious function than simply mourning a dead God, producing instead a body of work of great spiritual depth *and* corporeal embodiment. This is even true for *Written on the Body*, which as Chapter 5 will show, has an apophatic negative theology in the form of its 'gender undeclared' narrator *and* a fully embodied interest in the body of the beloved Louise – another example of Winterson's interest in the other. Where many theologies leave the body behind in the quest for the transcendent, Winterson's work approaches the divine through the material body of the self and other, and most especially the beloved. This fleshly theology problematizes any easy separation between secular and religious, sacred and profane, instead finding in the encounter with alterity a profound and important form of spiritual practice.

I argue, therefore, that Winterson is one contemporary writer whose work draws our attention to the religious in important and provocative ways. Although she was raised in the Pentecostal faith that we see dramatized in *Oranges Are Not the Only Fruit*, Winterson's work is not easily reducible to any particular version of Christianity, and although she has a particular partiality for Catholicism (the French and Italian characters in *The Passion* are Catholic, as is the defrocked priest Handel in *Art & Lies*), ultimately Winterson is not easily categorizable as strictly a Christian writer. Her Jewish characters in *Gut Symmetries* show one notable departure from Christianity, although it is more in her attention to the experiential that Winterson steps beyond the bounds of Christianity. As literary critic Terry Wright puts it, 'Winterson can no longer sign up to official church doctrines but clearly continues to find the Bible of great value'.[39]

Instead, her writing may be seen as gesturing to the phenomenological experience of religion, one that crosses boundaries between faiths, and between belief and unbelief. For the excessive *may* be an encounter with the divine – or it may not – and, ultimately, there is no way to verify the truth of the subjective experience of the sacred. Winterson is far less interested in the atheist discussion of religion as harmful or pernicious than with religion's power in creating sublime experience and its transformative effects on its subjects. Encountering the sublime dimension of otherness may occur in religion, in literature, in art, in music and in love for Winterson, and each plays a significant role in her work. And *that* is what should excite us and trouble us: to witness a radical body of work by a significant modern writer, wrestling with the questions of faith and practice and passion in a modern world.

1

'I Love Both of Them': Queer Love and the Religious in *Oranges Are Not the Only Fruit*

Eve Kosofsky Sedgwick famously began her foundational work *Epistemology of the Closet* with the declaration that much of Western culture is 'structured – indeed, fractured – by a chronic, now endemic crisis of homo/heterosexual definition, indicatively male, dating from the end of the nineteenth century'.[1] Along with anti-abortion politics, the homo/heterosexual fracture has been one of the most powerful ways in which Christian belief is articulated in the United States and other Anglophonic countries over the last thirty years. The forceful homophobia of the Catholic Church's clergy, the Church of the Later Day Saints, the Southern Baptist Convention and other evangelical groups has made opposition to gay rights a significant, perhaps dominant, position among religious conservatives. In such contexts, homosexuality is defined as always-already secular, with heterosexuality sanctified under the sign of the religious. Yet, although there are strong links between secular and queer and religious and straight, there is also a strong body of work from writers who problematize the easy conflation of these terms. As I have established in the Introduction, Winterson's work is a particularly compelling example of not only what we might call post-secular writing, but also queer and feminist writing.

Critical approaches to Winterson's work have largely been in the form of feminist (especially lesbian-feminist) and postmodern/post-structuralist theories, with queer theories emerging from the conversation between the two.² This substantial body of criticism has examined Winterson's distinctive use of language, her invocations of gender, sexuality and desire, and the identity politics implications of her writing as a female writer, a lesbian and so on, yet the notable religious element to her work remains relatively under-theorized. Her most famous work, 1985's autobiographical novel *Oranges Are Not the Only Fruit*, stages the definitional conflict between religion and homosexuality, only to collapse it. In the novel, the teenage Jeanette falls in love with another girl in her evangelical church and, after a failed exorcism, is eventually expelled from her community as a result of her insistence upon not merely homosexuality's acceptability, but its holiness.

In its alliance of sexuality with the sacred, *Oranges Are Not the Only Fruit* comes close to what Argentinian theologian Marcella Althaus-Reid has called an 'indecent theology'.³ The analysis of gendered and sexual relationships to the sacred by feminist and queer theorists is important for the study of Winterson's text, for sacred and sexual are profoundly entangled in her work. In *The Queer God*, Althaus-Reid argues that 'belief systems are organized around people's bodies, and people's bodies in relationships, and in sexual relationships'.⁴ She argues that religious belief is inextricably linked to sexual, gendered, raced and classed ideologies that are mediated through the body. Or as theologians Chris Boesel and Catherine Keller put it, 'divinity comes [...] encumbered by the projection of all manner of finite images derived from our bodily life: images of a lord or warrior, a friend or father, a humanoid love, and minimally, an inconspicuous personal pronoun [that is, he]'.⁵ So the kinds of bodies in the Christian imaginary, most especially that of God 'himself', are organized normatively, produced as discursive power along the lines of heterosexist, racist, misogynistic and imperialist thought. As well as the idealized bodies of the spiritual, aberrant bodies are produced that become formally constituted outside of the purvey of theology, and indeed outside of religion and religious communities in general (or, less formally, relegated unacknowledged inside the closet). To put it bluntly: queer bodies are rarely framed as holy bodies.[6]

Oranges Are Not the Only Fruit is framed as a religious text itself, each chapter is named after a book of the Hebrew Bible, beginning with Genesis and ending, significantly, in Ruth. Jeanette's mother Louie is described as being 'Old Testament through and through. Not for her the meek and paschal Lamb, she was out there, up front with the prophets, and much given to sulking under trees when the appropriate destruction didn't materialise.'[7] Susana Onega argues convincingly that Jeanette's birth in *Oranges* mirrors the birth of Christ in the New Testament, 'thus equating Jeanette's prescribed role as Evangelical preacher with Jesus' mission to save the world.'[8] Given this emphasis on the law, it is interesting to note that there is no exact prohibition against lesbianism in the Torah. The infamous verse in Leviticus 18:22 refers only to male homosexuality – 'thou shalt not lay with mankind as with womankind'. For Jewish feminist theologian Judith Plaskow, the narratives of Torah are mediated from the start by masculinist interpretative frameworks with the result that women are spoken about by men but never speaking. As she puts it, 'women's revelatory experiences are largely omitted from the sources; narratives are framed from an androcentric perspective; the law enforces women's subordination in the patriarchal family'.[9] Despite the gaps in the law, Jewish tradition nevertheless contains a substantial amount of homophobia directed at women (for instance, famed medieval rabbinical interpreter Rashi's commentary on the Talmud's Yevamot 76a on lesbianism, as well as comments by Moses Maimonides aka the rabbi Ramban). The absence of lesbianism from the holiest books of Judaism and Christianity has most certainly not meant an absence of homophobia.

In describing what is treated as a religious transgression – sin – Louie uses the term 'unnatural desires', a term which makes from nineteenth-century sexological taxonomies a vague gesture towards a plethora of aberrant sexual practices. We know from the historiographical work of the likes of Michel Foucault and David Halperin that ideas of 'the heterosexual' and 'the homosexual' as inherent identity-forming characteristics emerged in Europe in the nineteenth century. Foucault famously argued in the first volume of *The History of Sexuality* that 'the sodomite had been a temporary aberration, the homosexual was now a species'.[10] Winterson gestures towards this sexological lineage when her narrator mentions that her church had 'read Havelock Ellis and knew about Inversion',[11] a claim mocked by the narrator who even as a child 'knew that a woman was as far from a [male] homosexual as a rhinoceros'.[12] Of course, the primary referent of 'unnatural desires' in *Oranges* remains homosexuality; the invert, the masturbating child and the zoophile are nowhere to be seen. Instead, homosexuality has become, as Sedgwick argues, a site of primary identity formation and cultural antagonism over the course of the twentieth century.

Here, as with other religious condemnations of homosexuality, secular forms of subjectivity formation come to inflect the religious law of acts. Homophobic articulations like 'hate the sin, love the sinner' swerve awkwardly between older formulations of the act-based sodomite and the modern homosexual, with even celibate gay-identified Christians facing discrimination in some churches. This language of 'nature' recalls the debate between Augustine and Justin of Eclamus in the fourth century about nature, albeit with a modern twist. Where Augustine held that spontaneous sexual desire was proof of original sin, Justin argued that 'natural sin does not exist'. Justin pointed out that 'God made bodies, distinguished the sexes, made genitalia, bestowed the affection through which bodies would be joined [...] and God made nothing evil'.[13] While Augustine's position on original sin was taken up by the church, over the course of modernity it has steadily lost ground as a form of 'common sense' in and out of churches. The naturalization of desire in general may be one of the effects of modern secularization, albeit still incompletely applied for homosexuality in particular.[14]

Religious rhetorics

But if the secular comes to infect the homophobia of religious communities, homosexuality for Winterson can be shown to be religious from the start. The homophobic sexological language of the church is rebutted with an individualized language based on emotion. Jeanette asks her girlfriend Melanie: "'Do you think this is an Unnatural Passion?" […] "Doesn't feel like it. According to Pastor Finch, that's awful.'" While, as Michelle Denby points out,[15] there is a certain kind of New Age individualized 'spirituality' apparent in this move towards the body and good feeling as the guarantor of truth, it's also worth noting the individualized nature of evangelical Christian protestations of faith (and indeed broader historical movements of Protestantism as Max Weber argued). From this angle, Winterson's individualization is more a mirror image of her community than exhibiting signs of the Eastern-influenced New Age. Jeanette articulates her desire through the religious, telling Melanie, 'I love you almost as much as I love the Lord',[16] while her later relationship with Katy 'did have a genuinely spiritual dimension'.[17]

Problematizing the idea of sexuality as a Fall, Jeanette defends herself with the refrain, 'to the pure all things are pure'. Her love, it is clear, is not a sin. Instead, it is through the language of religious oratory that queer desire is expressed in the novel. Denby points out that 'to the pure all things are pure', reverses St Paul's ideal of physical purity in 1 Corinthians 7 and Ephesians 5[18] – in particular, Ephesians 5:3, which states that 'among you there must not be even a hint of sexual immorality, or of any kind of impurity, or of greed, because these are improper for God's holy people'. Winterson here makes purity a facet not of refraining from behaviour (as in the equation between virginity and purity), but rather a state of mind. Purity is less the inherent characteristic of bodies and actions than of the quality of the relationship between the people involved.

Yet the argument proves to be unconvincing for the members of Jeanette's church. Onega notes that 'Jeanette must fight the religious community alone, armed only with her trust in God's words'.[19] At her exorcism, Pastor Finch frames religious devotion as mutually exclusive from same-sex love. Jeanette says, 'I love her' (meaning Melanie), to which Finch replies 'then you do not love the Lord'. Jeanette rebuts this opposition, saying 'yes I love both of them',[20] a statement which I take as emblematic of the refusing of a binary between the religious/secular. Here, as in other places in the novel, the queer relationship to God becomes narrativized as a kind of love affair, an ultimately failed one less because of the divine than the mediation of a church which is shown to be sinful.

Queer prophets

One of the ways in which Winterson's work collapses boundaries and hierarchies is in its adoption of a prophetic voice. Onega has argued convincingly that Winterson can be considered part of a broader visionary tradition in English literature that stretches from William Blake and the Romantic poets, and culminates with the modernists (Eliot and Joyce in particular). Indeed, as Onega rightly notes, Winterson's work is profoundly interested in the role of the prophet, especially in *Oranges*.

Where a simplistic understanding of the role of a prophet often includes solely their clairvoyance of future events, the Biblical prophets were much more complicated in function. As Rabbi Abraham Heschel writes, 'the prophet is not only a prophet. He is also poet, preacher, patriot, statesman, social critic, moralist.'[21] Each one of these functions is put into play in proclaiming the prophet's message. Heschel talks about the psychological make-up of the prophet: a sensitivity to evil, an iconoclast, a flouter of all forms of authority and common practice, a pathos for the life of God, austere and compassionate at the same time. The prophet condemns the evils of their society and the complacency that allows them to take place. A prophet is someone who proclaims fidelity to their ideals, and bemoans the consequences of a lack of faith. He or she talks at 'an octave too high',[22] with a message so far from the norms of civil society that it appears to be another language altogether. Yet, as Heschel writes, 'prophetic utterance is rarely cryptic, suspended between God and man; it is urging, alarming, forcing onward, as if the words gushed forth from the heart of God, seeking entrance to the heart and mind of man, carrying a summons as well as an involvement'.[23] One cannot be unmoved by the prophet's message; it is the unmoved and hypocritical that the prophet targets.

It is not only the Hebrew Bible that features prophetic language. Northrop Frye argues that, although it also takes in metaphor, abstraction and descriptive language, the Bible primarily functions as 'kerygma, proclamation'.[24] Kerygma is the preaching of the New Testament to the unconverted, to pagans. Like the language of Heschel's prophets, kerygma makes demands upon its listeners, demanding faith and action alike. Kerygma in modern thought is primarily associated with the theologian Rudolf Bultmann, who opposes it as myth.

We can see this prophetic voice of Winterson's most clearly in *Oranges*, where she takes in the evangelizing of her Pentecostal upbringing. Louie, the mother of Jeanette, the heroine of the novel, is a figure of Biblical proportions, who draws strongly on the prophetic tradition in the way she imagines evangelical outreach to the non-believers.[25] She flouts the social norms of the small Lancashire town in which they live, antagonizing her neighbours and ignoring the concerns of Jeanette's teachers about her child's overzealous religiousness. Jeanette's mother Louie lists her enemies, praying vengeance upon them. Yet hers is no nihilism, but rather a black-and-white worldview in which sin is ever-present and the world is ripe for conversion. Jeanette and her mother climb a hill at the end of their street, which looks down upon the entire town in which they live: 'We stood on the hill and my mother said, "This world is full of sin." We stood on the hill and my mother said, "You can change the world."'[26] Similarly, Jeanette's other female role model Elsie 'liked the prophets' and enjoys a needlework sampler that Jeanette sews with a quote from Jeremiah: 'the summer is ended and we are not yet saved' (Jer. 8:20). The work of the prophet, of evangelizing to the unconverted, is all pervasive in Jeanette's world, with her mother preparing her for a life of evangelizing in Africa (modelled on St John Rivers in her mother's beloved, truncated version of *Jane Eyre*).

Yet this attention to the role of a prophet is not without ambivalence. When Jeanette is discovered for a second time with a female lover, the pastor claims that it is Jeanette's preaching that has caused her to stray from the path of heterosexuality. Usurping the role of men, spiritually is suggested to be the cause of Jeanette's sexual usurping of masculinity – 'having taken on a man's ways in other ways [that is, preaching] I had flouted God's law and tried to do it sexually'.[27] So, for a woman like Jeanette to fully inhabit the role of the prophet becomes a source of conflict for the evangelical church, precisely because of its success, for as Jeanette notes, 'some of us could preach and quite plainly, in my case, the church was full of it'.[28] The conflation between gender and sexuality makes a kind of cultural sense, for as Judith Butler has argued, in a heteronormative patriarchy, 'the internal coherence of either gender, man or woman, thereby requires [...] a stable and oppositional heterosexuality'.[29] In loving a woman, Jeanette's gender has become problematized, and vice versa – by preaching, Jeanette breaks out of the restrictive gendered role of a woman in patriarchy, mirroring her sexual rebellion from the church.

Although the evangelical world of her mother and Elsie is shown to be limited and harmful, Jeanette nevertheless takes from it a prophetic intensity. As Heschel has argued, the prophet is an iconoclast who flouts authority, just as Jeanette flouts the combined authority of her mother and the male pastor. Jeanette reflects:

> I could have been a priest instead of a prophet. The priest has a book with the words set out. Old words, known words, words of power [...] The prophet has no book. The prophet is a voice that cries in the wilderness, full of sounds that do not always set into meaning. The prophets cry out because they are troubled by demons.[30]

Jeanette eschews the comfort of what she terms the priest for that of the more uncertain path of the prophet.

But Winterson's prophetic voice is not merely limited to ventriloquizing Christian evangelicals. It is arguable that, in her work, she is a secular prophet, calling passionately for truth, love and passion itself. In her interviews, Winterson has talked of the 'sanctified space' of the book, and the parallels between the persuasive rhetoric of the preacher and that of the writer. The difference between the preacher and the writer for Winterson is that 'the artist does it in its own right, for its own sake, not for some higher purpose, not for God'.[31] And yet, it is easy to see the artist's invocation of otherness to be continually on the edge of the sacred, adjoining, supplementing, replacing.

For Winterson, the world is enchanted in the Weberian sense, full of magic and mystery. As Heschel puts it, 'others may suffer from the terror of cosmic aloneness; the prophet is overwhelmed by the grandeur of divine presence'.[32] Jeanette's queer desires are tied together with her form of religious oratory – she is one of the church's most successful preachers. As an evangelist, Louie sees the world as available for conversion, preparing her daughter for a career of preaching. Jeanette 'learned to interpret the signs and wonders that the unbeliever might never understand. "You'll need to when you're out there on the mission field," she [Louie] reminded me.'[33]

Louie and Jeanette listen to the BBC World Service, which gives details of religious conversions in the 'Missionary Report':

> The Missionary Report was a great trial to me because our mid-day meal depended on it. If it went well, no deaths and lots of converts, my mother cooked a joint. If the Godless had proved not only stubborn but murderous, my mother spent the rest of the morning listening to the Jim Reeves Devotional Selection, and we had to have boiled eggs and toast soldiers.[34]

This close attention to the religious shows the ways in which even the most mundane elements of life have been sacralized by Louie to contain evangelical content, an enchantment which Jeanette shares, even as she takes this into queerer places.

Jeanette's prophetic role as a preacher ultimately proves to be a source of conflict for the evangelical church. In response to her outing, the church decides 'the real problem [...] was going against the teachings of St Paul, and allowing women power in the church. Our branch of the church had never thought about it, we'd always had strong women, and the women organised everything. Some of us could preach and quite plainly, in my case, the church was full because of it.'[35] There is a clear conflict between the misogynistic and homophobic symbols of the church – the official line inherited from St Paul – and the unofficial culture of the church, which makes full use of the talents of its women.

While this situation is obviously partly a further confusion of gender and sexuality, the entanglement of Jeanette's religious language with her sexuality marks a threat that necessitates the silencing of all of the church's women. In the end the homophobic measures the church takes against its female preachers unwittingly weaken it, with an even more devastating show of 'unnatural desires' from a male Reverend, siphoning off the money raised for missionary efforts to pay off his gambling debts and almost bankrupting the church to pay his estranged wife maintenance. Louie notes bleakly that he 'lives in sin' with his girlfriend.[36]

Yet, if the church has declined, Winterson closes with a resolutely religious image. The final chapter is titled Ruth, a telling move given that the exact nature of Ruth and Naomi's relationship has long been the subject of speculation and heated scholarly debate, especially among queer theologians. Ruth's vow to Naomi has been commonly read at marriage and civil union ceremonies, gay and straight, as a statement of intense commitment. Evidence for homoeroticism has been found in a reading of 1:14, where the Hebrew word used for 'clave' is the same as that used for marriage in Genesis 2:24.[37] Even putting aside those queer hints, Ruth provides a model of supportive female community in which men are largely irrelevant. In *Oranges*, the novel ends with a kind of resolution for Jeanette's mother Louie, who has taken to the airwaves after the failure of her church. Jeanette muses that 'I seemed to have run in a great circle, and met myself again on the starting line'.[38]

Nevertheless, towards the end of the novel, Jeanette laments the loss of existential security that the God of the church had provided her:

> [W]here was God now, with heaven full of astronoughts, and the Lord overthrown? I miss God. I miss the company of someone utterly loyal. I still don't think of God as my betrayer. The servants of God, yes, but servants by the very nature betray. I miss God who was my friend. I don't even know if God exists, but I do know if God is your emotional role model, very few human relationships will match up to it.[39]

Cast out from the church, it is hard for Jeanette to maintain the easy and simplistic belief in the evangelical God, and she must look for

God in the immanent, in her relationships with other human beings – primarily, in sexual relationships with other women. 'I would cross seas and suffer sunstroke and give away all I have, but not for a man',[40] she states. A queer approach to the sacred has none of the ease in which heterosexual and gender-normative bodies sink into their homophobic traditions. As Sara Ahmed puts it, 'heteronormativity functions as a form of public comfort by allowing bodies to extend into spaces that have already taken their shape. Those spaces are lived as comfortable as they allow bodies to fit in; the surfaces of social space are already impressed upon by the shapes of such bodies.'[41] Instead, queer bodies have felt discomfort, rubbing against the grain of many (but not all, admittedly) religious traditions, practices and texts. A queer sacred like Winterson's must draw selectively from the tradition of religious oratory from which it emerges, 'taking the joy and comfort and ignoring the rest',[42] as she puts it in *The Passion*. Little wonder that Winterson's work is post-secular, less a religious canon of dogma and rigid practice than a supple rereading of the Christian tradition.

Conclusion

Oranges Are Not the Only Fruit raises serious questions about the way in which we conceptualize sin in the present day, as much a form of identity formation (categorical sinfulness) as action. There is no necessary reason for this particular 'sin' to assume the prominence that it does. While the attempt to remove Jeanette's 'sin' from the community initially galvanizes in a familiar scapegoating dynamic, it ultimately weakens the church and glosses over more serious moral failures. There is no space in this particular evangelical community for Jeanette to be a lesbian preacher, even as her language suggests it. So, we might wish to ask ourselves what it is that has made homosexuality historically considered necessarily sinful, and why religious understandings of homosexuality are univocal compared to the polyphony of heterosexual sex, love, relationships and conduct that may or may not be considered sinful. The notion that all homosexual encounters are of themselves sinful regardless of quality or violation of other religious laws seems reductive at best. In other words, we may well wish to consider why we continue to speak of hetero- and homosexuality in the singular, when there are clearly heterosexualities and homosexualities, bisexualities that cut through both and other forms of sexuality proliferating – and that each of these may well occupy a different place in the innocence/sin binary.

Jeanette muses to herself that 'it all seemed to hinge around the fact that I loved the wrong sort of people. Right sort of people except for one; romantic love for a woman was a sin.'[43] Winterson's novel profoundly destabilizes any easy demarcation between sacred and profane, religion and sexuality, sinfulness and holiness. Instead, in Winterson the heterosexist cultural organization of desires and bodies of Christian theology and practice is thoughtfully and productively reworked into new configurations, infusing the prophetic tradition with new blood. In doing so, Winterson raises profoundly spiritual – and still controversial – questions about embodied experience and the sacred imaginary.

As Althaus-Reid provocatively puts it, 'let us suppose [...] that God is outside traditions; that God transgresses sexual traditions, and [...] God imagines new traditions all the time. Why not God the faggot? Why not Mary the Queer of Heaven?'[44] The Christian imaginary is so thoroughly heterosexual and gender normative that Althaus-Reid's questions may shock, even appal, many Christians.[45] Heterosexuals take for granted the normality of their lives reflected back to them as ideals – in advertisements, television and film, political discussions and churches. Faced with the homophobia of religious traditions, queers like Jeanette in *Oranges* may wonder whether the 'demon' of homosexuality is worth living with – or conversely, if Christianity (and God) can be held onto in the face of heterosexual indifference or hostility. In *Oranges*, Jeanette leaves God behind, missing him, in a form of Sartre's 'God shaped hole'. Winterson's writing poses similarly difficult, but still surprising, questions about the sacredness of queer, and lesbian, experience. Oranges are not the only fruit, just as heterosexuals are not the only Christians.

2

'Colours and Folly': Retelling the Noah Story in *Boating for Beginners*

God chose what is foolish in the world to shame the wise; God chose what is weak in the world to shame the strong.

(1 Cor. 1:27 (New Revised Standard Version))

Boating for Beginners, Winterson's second novel, has attracted little interest from readers and critics alike, with almost no critical writing on the text besides a few reviews.[1] Indeed, the novel has often been excluded from Winterson's canon, with readers jumping from *Oranges Are Not the Only Fruit* to *The Passion*. On her website, Winterson describes it as a 'comic book with pictures' that was 'never intended as a second novel'.[2] In fact, Winterson notes that the novel was 'written for money in 6 weeks'. Written in a broader tone than Winterson's other early work, it is unsurprising therefore that *Boating* has struggled to find an audience. Less ambitious formally than its predecessor, *Boating* nevertheless is interesting for our purposes in examining the religious import of Winterson's corpus, for in its retelling of the Noah story the novel is Winterson's most direct extended encounter with the Bible.

Written in 1987, *Boating for Beginners* takes the story of Noah from Genesis and gleefully reimagines the text as a postmodern fairy tale. Here, in Nineveh – a town with more in common with contemporary Britain than with the ancient Middle East – Noah is a tele-evangelist who accidentally created God by mixing electricity with a chocolate gateau. Traumatized by this incident, Noah tells his followers to avoid frozen food. At God's command, he builds an ark to house himself, his girlfriend Bunny Mix (a romance novelist), his sons, their wives and, of course, two animals of every kind. Meanwhile, a rag-tag group of women, including an amateur psychologist/plastic surgeon, a Northrop Frye-reading receptionist and a transgender woman, try to prevent the devastation of everything they know – or at least to survive it. As should be clear from this description, *Boating for Beginners* is not a text with a tremendous amount of reverence for its origins in the Hebrew Bible. Yet it is a text whose playful attitude towards the Bible conceals a more serious interest in religion that connects to Winterson's more serious, weightier work.

In a poignant passage, the narrator of *Boating* makes the following comments about religion in general that can be taken as something of a mission statement for the novel:

> It's very potent, that Punch and Judy show book [i.e. the Bible]. The Romantics didn't need it because they found their own fire; but almost every quasi-revolt has gone back to it, because when the heart revolts it wants things that cannot possibly be factual. Robes and incense and larger-than-life and miracles and heroes. It's all there, it's heart-food, and the more we deprive ourselves of colours and folly, the more attractive that now legitimate folly will become.[3]

Here Winterson is quite explicitly making an argument about the role of religion in the human psyche. Religion and myth – and it is questionable whether there is truly a meaningful difference between the two for Winterson[4] – feed the human soul in their very irrationality, giving us something that mere reason cannot.

Although Winterson is talking in the language of basic humanism, there is a more profound theological point being made in her invocation of 'colours and folly'. *Boating* is a text in which various kinds of folly are ventured, and the necessity of that folly is affirmed as the precondition for not merely faith, but meaningful existence. The trappings of religion (robes, incense etc.) play an important role for those like protagonist Gloria whose hearts do revolt from the status quo, and although, in using the example of the Romantics, Winterson allows for the possibility of art as revolt, it is clear that religion is the most potent form of folly for her in this instance (a position that she will reverse later in *Art & Lies*).

Although the Noah story is a Jewish story, there is something quite Christian in the idea of a divine folly. Philosopher and theologian John Caputo in *The Weakness of God* has argued that the Kingdom of God is an anarchistic one, in which the first becomes last, the last becomes first, and the divine wedding feast finds guests from the streets just as much as the chosen few. As Caputo puts it:

> One of the most interesting events, or laws of the event, in the New Testament is that the out are in and the in are out. The characters in the kingdom are a cast of outcasts, of outsiders: sinners, lost sheep, lost coins, lost and prodigal sons, tax collectors, prostitutes, Samaritans, lepers, the lame, the possessed, the children. A list that we today could easily update: gays and lesbians, illegal immigrants, unwed mothers, the HIV-positive, drug addicts, prisoners, and, after 9/11, Arabs. Everyone who is outside, outlawed and outclassed – in short, everyone who is just plain out and should stay out of sight.[5]

Caputo invokes the topsy-turvy world of Lewis Carroll's more than a few times throughout the text, but I think that Winterson's writing in general – and *Boating for Beginners* in particular – arguably shows those same anarchistic qualities.

Appropriately for my analysis of a Jewish story retold by a post-Christian writer, it is important to note that Caputo's anarchic take on the New Testament, its code scrambling and reversals, is also drawn from his reading of the twentieth-century Jewish philosopher Emmanuel Levinas, for whom ethics is his great theme. Caputo takes from Levinas the idea that it is in meeting the stranger, the other, that the divine manifests itself. In drawing on Levinas, as well as his muse Jacques Derrida, the deconstructionist Caputo creates a Judeo-Christian theological methodology that does not simply sublate Judaism into Christianity, but rather refigures Christian theology quite profoundly through an encounter with post-metaphysical Jewish thought. Caputo, like Winterson, disrupts easy binary boundaries between Jewish and Christian, moving out towards a more generalized post-secular form of religious thought. This inattention to disciplinary boundaries may be thought of as folly too.

Indeed, Winterson's novel scrambles codes of acceptability, with the most holy character of the Biblical narrative Noah shown to be indifferent to the mass deaths of the flooded world, while a trio of women (including a transgender woman) are shown to be more compassionate. The protagonist Gloria is an unlikely heroine, moving aimlessly through life and guided more by the writings of Northrop Frye than by the Bible (in a self-referential twist, Gloria refers to Frye's theories from *The Great Code*, written about the Bible as a form of literature). Although her mother names her Gloria 'after the Glory Crusade, and it was Mrs Munde's one hope that her daughter should serve the Unpronounceable in some way',[6] it appears at first glance that Gloria is a far cry from the larger-than-life characters in the Bible – not so much a sinner as merely unexceptional. Grappling with the overwhelming presence of her evangelical mother, Gloria struggles to define herself in any meaningful way. 'You don't belong to a union and you don't know anything about the transience of existence! No wonder you haven't got on in the world. You're a fool to yourself'[7] she is told. Gloria's folly drives the narrative, with her journey from naivety and a lack of self-knowledge to wisdom.

Gloria is an interesting choice for a protagonist in a rewrite of the Noah story. As Winterson is clearly well aware, there are few female characters in the Bible, and fewer still occupying the role of protagonist. Jewish feminist Judith Plaskow has argued in her landmark book

Standing Again on Sinai that, in the Hebrew Bible, women are spoken about by men, and the narratives of Torah are mediated from the start by masculinist interpretative frameworks. As Plaskow puts it, 'women's revelatory experiences are largely omitted from the sources; narratives are framed from an androcentric perspective; the law enforces women's subordination in the patriarchal family'.[8] In the Hebrew Bible, women listen at the door, like Sarah in Genesis 18:10, or are not mentioned at all. So, Winterson is profoundly reworking the text in making female characters central to her plot. In *Boating for Beginners* she is writing back the holy text from a female perspective, which was excluded from the Noah story in Genesis, making a feminist intervention into the masculinist world of religion.

This sense of writing from the margins that we get from the characterization of Gloria is intensified by Gloria's companions, especially Marlene, a transgender woman. Indeed, it is hard to think of an identity more 'out' of conventional codes of holiness than a transgender woman – after all, many (if not all) modern Christians[9] from the Pope downwards have condemned the transgender community as innately sinful – but Winterson's characterization of Marlene, while ridiculous in some ways (this is, after all, a comic novel), is drawn with some sympathy as a loyal friend to Gloria. Desi, one of Noah's daughters-in-law and the third of the novel's heroines, summarizes the book's approach to Marlene's difference[10] (and plans to re-attach a penis to her body 'for decoration') with a vague but understanding aside to Gloria. 'There are always people who […] whatever you can think of. Whatever combination, innovation or desperation, there are always people who […].'[11] Winterson's female characters have a live-and-let-live ethos akin to the inclusive and diverse modern multicultural state, after feminism and LGBT liberation. It is this which is destroyed in the watery grave of the divinely mandated flood, although not without leaving some important traces of the women of the story and their divine anarchy.

Of course, it is important to note that the Biblical narrative and its interpretations have painted Noah with some divine folly of his own. There is something profoundly irrational about Noah's fidelity to God's command. According to Midrash – the Jewish stories that expand the narratives of the Torah – Noah drew out the building of the ark for 120 years. For over a century, he worked on the ark, so that 'on being asked, "Why are you doing this?" he replied, "The Lord of the Universe has informed me that He will bring a Flood in the world"' (Genesis Rabbah 30:7).[12] It is hard to imagine a more ridiculous way to spend a year, let alone a century. And yet, alone of his generation, Noah is righteous, obeying God's command. It is no wonder then that Genesis says that Noah 'walked with God' (6:9).

Winterson is well aware of the folly of Noah, parodying the relationship of the believer to the divine by making God a sentient cloud made from chocolate cake. As a tele-evangelist, Noah knowingly deploys the colours and folly of religion to ridiculous effect, writing books on behalf of God with titles like *Genesis, or How I Did It*. The food purity codes of *kashrut* (kosher) are re-imagined as a vendetta against frozen food. Noah is, in fact, a hypocrite who denounces freezers but whose 'preaching activity is inextricably linked to the use of the "mass" media on which he relies for the success of the broadcast he's prepared in collaboration with God'.[13] The avarice of some members of the Christian Right is parodied in the faith of Noah's son Ham, who owns a chain of restaurants:

> I own those stores for His Sake, not my own. He has guided me through the money markets and the loopholes in the Health and Safety Regulations because he is more than YAHWEH, the God of Love, he is YAHWEH the Omnipotent Stockbroker and YAHWEH the Omniscient Lawyer. (Praise Him.)[14]

There is little that is holy in the workplace violations of health and safety regulations by corporations, or in refusing to pay workers a fair wage, and certainly none of the divine anarchy with which Caputo characterizes the Kingdom. We can therefore contrast the anarchistic holiness of Winterson's women with that of Noah and his followers, who in *Boating* are not so much holy fools as self-interested opportunists.[15]

In the end, however, the folly in *Boating for Beginners* is that of God, who desires the destruction of mankind simply so that the narrative can be rewritten so as to have included God from the start: 'Once we've got rid of the old world we're going to have a lot of work to do, and if you lot don't come up with some ideas to make me coherent to future generations I'll take your ocean-going ark and smash it.'[16] God's folly, paradoxically, is not the passionately coloured folly that Winterson so often writes glowingly of in her corpus, but rather a folly designed for power and control – the God of orthodoxy so beloved of fundamentalists everywhere. As a missive from God in a cloud puts it: 'GOD IS LOVE, DON'T MESS WITH ME.'[17] As Wright notes, 'the Yahweh of this novel is a monster of power, totally lacking in the qualities of compassion, justice and mercy ascribed to the Yahweh of the Bible as a whole.'[18]

While Genesis is quite clear that God is motivated by the 'evil of man', which was 'great in the earth' (6:5), Winterson's Nineveh is far from evil. Instead, it is drawn with the banal consumerism and competing ideologies of the modern world in broadly comic tones – from the refrigerator-hating irrationality of Noah's followers to romance-novel fans and socialist theatre. God's homicidal act of destroying the world, Winterson seems to suggest, is as unfair and irrational as those apocalyptic Christians who long for the end of the world today. Folly, Winterson suggests, is a deeply ambivalent experience whose effects are manifold.

The 'organic philosopher' and cleaning lady Doris has a conversation with an orange demon who Winterson has recycled from *Oranges Are Not the Only Fruit*:

'[H]eroes', she mused. 'Why does the world need heroes?'

'Obvious', said the orange demon, poking its head round her duster. 'The impulse to worship is impossible to eradicate. Even the most prosaic have to worship something [...] If we don't give her [Gloria] something real to worship she'll end up like her mother. An emotional vacuum is a dangerous thing.'[19]

Here Winterson suggests that the desire to venerate is an inherent desire for humanity that will attach to anyone or anything – a perspective that psychoanalysts like Freud would see as prolonging the 'illusions' of religion in another form.[20] And yet, Winterson is arguing that there are real things that one can worship, and in *Boating* it is clear that female companionship might be one of them.

Creation and the ocean

Boating for Beginners ends with an interesting scene in which almost all of the female characters in the book gather in boats of their own. It is a scene with some surprising theological resonances, which an examination of some recent feminist theology will help to draw out. In feminist theologian Catherine Keller's wonderful book *Face of the Deep*,[21] she discusses the contradictory ways in which the ocean has been conceptualized in Western culture. From the very beginnings of Western culture, the depths of the ocean have been suggested to contain both awe-inspiring wonders and monsters. While the surface of the ocean has been well and truly explored (no longer is it possible to insert 'here be dragons' into a nautical map), the depths of the ocean rarely have been plumbed. What lies beneath has been ignored and, at worst, vilified as a source of horror. The highly gendered image of the ocean is a site of both creation and chaos – a bifurcation with profoundly religious significance in general, and especially in relation to the watery Noah narrative.

Keller argues powerfully that cultural bifurcation about the ocean commences right at the beginning of the Bible in Genesis, with the Christian theological tradition of *creatio ex nihilio* affirming the God of power and empire instead of affirming its watery origins. In the *creatio ex nihilio*, God creates the earth from nothing, a reading that Keller argues ignores a more profound – and feminist – way of seeing creation as wet, messy and female. Keller argues that creation was (is and remains) instead a *creatio ex profundis* as she calls it, a creation from the depths. She notes that the 'earth' in Genesis 1:2 is formless, dark and wet. The ocean pre-exists land, and instead vacillates between substance and absence, form and formlessness. God then creates night and day (Gen. 1:4–5), and then divides the waters into two, where one above is called Heaven, and that below remains water. Oddly enough, given that 'earth' has become synonymous with land, it is not until the third day of creation in Genesis 1:9 that dry land appears.

The formless and empty aspect of Genesis 1:2, as Keller points out, has been a problem for Jewish and Christian writers for millennia. Many writers have simply skipped over the 'churning, complicating darkness'[22] of the second verse, moving from the majestic and powerful opening to the creation of light in verse 3. Augustine struggles with the passage in his *Confessions*, finding that 'formless matter entirely without feature'[23] preceded the division into darkness and light, earth and ocean. Yet this provides a problem, for 'if it was to be there first, in order to be the vehicle for all these visible, composite forms, what can have been its origin?'[24] Where did the formless matter come from, and when was it created? Augustine is forced to a number of incomplete, problematic conclusions. First, he postulates that God created the matter before creation proper began, an unnarrativized supplementary creation that inadvertently supplants that of Genesis 1:2.[25] Second, given his difficulty in reconciling the passage, Augustine is forced to affirm the plurality of interpretation. Right from the beginning, then, as Derrida has said apropos Edmond Jabés, 'God contradicts himself [sic] already.'[26]

Nevertheless, despite these knotty problems, Genesis 1:2 became the theological backing for the Christian *creatio ex nihilo* doctrine, where God creates the earth out of nothingness. The *creatio ex nihilo* tries to draw a clear dividing line in creation, removing Augustine's 'formless matter' to begin with 'nothing but the pure and simple presence of God the Creator'.[27] God is affirmed as all-powerful, all-knowing and, most importantly, as the original origin. The chaos of creation cannot co-exist with God alone. This, as Caputo points out, is a gradual historical development, for 'to say that Elohim [God] makes something out of nothing [would have been] a puzzling notion indeed to anyone in Babylonia, to anyone at all before the second century C.E.'.[28] It is only from the second century in Iraneus to the fourth century that Christian theologians began to solidify the doctrine. 'The idea of a creation from nothing rather than a formation from formlessness only gradually ensconced itself in Christian common sense.'[29]

The full extent of the gendered implications of the *creatio ex nihilo* therefore becomes clear when we consider the kinds of fears that coalescence around the ocean. Keller points us towards one of Luce Irigaray's lesser-known books, *Marine Lover of Friedrich Nietzsche*, in which Irigaray mimes the historical equation of the ocean with femaleness, with the feminine and with childbirth. Addressing her writing ostensibly to Nietzsche, she says, 'it is to the earth that you preach fidelity. And forgetfulness of your birth.'[30] Irigaray condemns Nietzsche's idea of the eternal return, finding in it a masculine nostalgia for the womb that remains predicated on patrilineal father-son relationships. She says: 'Your whole will, your eternal recurrence, are these anything other than the dream of one who neither wants to have been born, nor to continue being born, at every instant, of a female other? Does your joy in becoming not result from annihilating her from whom you are tearing yourself away?'[31] The masculine movement away from the ocean, Irigaray suggests, is a movement away from the mother, away from bodies and matter. Ironically, it is a movement away from the earthiness through which female bodies are coded in patriarchal discourse.[32] In Keller's reading of Irigaray, the defence of the oceanic matter forms a critique of the kind of gendered amnesia that motivates the *creatio ex nihilio*.

Indeed, Irigaray suggests that the fear of the sea is partly a metaphysical dread. She says, 'there is no peril greater than the sea. Everything is constantly moving and remains eternally in flux'.[33] The metaphysics of materiality privileges solid over liquid, land over sea. Augustine tries to picture the formlessness of Genesis 1:2, imagining 'not something without form, but some shape so monstrous and grotesque that if I were to see it, my sense would recoil'.[34] Formless matter provokes fear simply because it is, because of its liminal space between being and not-being, visibility and invisibility, sex and sexlessness. The sea, therefore, brings with it the danger of dissolution, of the solid breaking down into the liquid. As with Julia Kristeva's work, that which is permeable, leaky, liquid is gendered female.[35] The fear of a dissolution caused by the ocean, of its flux and fluidity, is a fear not merely of the creative potential of (some) women, but of a deeply ingrained cultural sense of the instability of female bodies and femininity.

Water in the Noah story can be seen in both its destructive (tehomophobic) and creative (tehomophilic) senses. The Noah narrative often has been read as a rewriting of the Genesis creation story, in which God essentially resets creation, and tries again. In *Boating*, God resets the world so as to control the narrative of the creation of the world. 'Why don't I flood the place and we'll start again. We can change the book, put it out under a new cover, stick a bit on the price. No-one will know because they'll all be dead.'[36] The flood can be seen in this sense as a means to an end, for power and control. Here, God tries to rewrite history as the creator of the world – in other words, *creatio ex nihilo*. God's attempt to control the creation narrative writes out women and, paradoxically, the watery female-coded *creatio ex profoundis* of the face of the deep of Genesis 1.

It is therefore deeply significant that Winterson's characters conclude *Boating for Beginners* on the sea, together. Where the official narrative of Noah records only the ark, Winterson's rewriting sees a marginal group of women in the ocean, preparing to make their way through the flood on canoes. The community of women that Winterson portrays in *Oranges Are Not the Only Fruit* re-emerges, this time less faithful, and more foolish. Gloria's struggle for self-expression has been successful by the end of the novel, so she says 'I feel I can continue after the flood [...] I can think, I can string sentences together and I hope one day to manage a whole paragraph without losing my theme.'[37] Her holy guide, Northrop Frye, floats by, past the group of women. The struggle to survive the water, for Gloria, has been profoundly creative, as well as comically ridiculous.

While many orthodox readings see the story as a cleansing water, a re-creation, Keller's writing – and Winterson's – allows us to re-imagine the depths of the waters as containing fathoms of female desire and struggle. In *Boating for Beginners*, both tehomophobic and tehomophilic senses co-mingle – the destructive storm of God, Noah and an androcentric history that has written out women, and the ambivalent, risky, messy ocean in which Winterson's female characters try to make their way. The section finishes with a quote from Song of Songs, 'many waters cannot quench love, neither can floods drown it' (8:7), which affirms the persistence of desire.

> Doris held out her cup. 'Here's to the future – a world of fridge freezers and poetry.'
> 'And Northrop Frye', put in Gloria.
> 'And anti-cellulite cream and disposable razors', cheered Marlene.
> 'And the day we rediscover champagne', said Desi.[38]

Gloria's desire for an inner life, Marlene's desire for hairless, cellulite-free thighs, Doris's desire for meaning, these may be small wishes, but important ones regardless. As long as people live, they desire, Winterson seems to be suggesting reading the Bible against itself. So, rather than their possible (probable?) deaths, we last see the female characters with cake and champagne, uncertain but brave, facing a new world without all the comforts of the old one. It is folly to strike out on one's own in a canoe in a flood, but an admirable kind of folly that cannot be destroyed by the power of orthodoxy.

Conclusion

Winterson concludes the novel with a postscript set in the present day, in which two archaeologists trek to the top of Mount Ararat and discover a piece of gopher wood. 'And all the papers jumped up and down, and all the Bible scholars said "We told you so" and all the born-again believers said, "Praise the Lord."'[39] But, although the official Noah narrative has been accepted by the world – and thus Noah and God's quest to rewrite history without any of the modernity of Winterson's Nineveh has succeeded, as we knew it must – the novel ends with one final joke. Gardener, one of the archaeologists, discovers a book written in a combination of Hebrew, Sanskrit and hieroglyphics, that 'if he hadn't known better he would have said it was part of a romance novel; and in the bit he had, the heroine was in the kitchen whipping up a mushroom soufflé'.[40] Moreover, he finds a letter that attests to Doris's survival, a message in a bottle that reads 'hey girls, I made it'.[41] Where the Biblical narrative appears to efface the presence of women from the world, Winterson here shows that traces of women still survive, in the ambivalent sea of creation and chaos.

The novel ends with Gardener pondering to himself: '"Where did it come from? Who wrote it? And Doris, who was she?" And he answers himself time and time again as he walks down English lanes watching the stars: "God only knows", he says, "God only knows."[42] Although the official Biblical narrative has prevailed, there remains a trace of holy anarchy, of the margins, of the ridiculousness of Bunny Mix's romance narratives, of Doris the organic philosopher, of the community of women in the watery depths of creation who the Bible has left out.

3

The Love Event in *The Passion*

I would like to return to the idea of passion raised by *Oranges Are Not the Only Fruit*, in another perhaps more universal way. Where *Oranges* is specifically the story of a lesbian *bildungsroman*, Winterson's work throughout the 1990s became more interested in bisexuality, although it retains sexual relationships between women as the source of much creativity for her characters. Sonya Andermahr argues compellingly that 'Winterson's project [...] has been the creation of a new language for the expression of sexual love, drawing on [...] the long tradition of Western quest romances.'[1] Clearly, one of the important thematics in Winterson's writing is passion.[2]

The Passion is written from the perspective of twin characters – Henri, a French cook in Napoleon's army, and Villanelle, a female card dealer at Venice's Casino with a penchant for cross-dressing. Henri's great passion is Napoleon himself, who he sees as a charismatic leader who has seduced the entire nation of France, while Villanelle's passion is for a woman she describes only as the Queen of Spades, a married woman who becomes Villanelle's lover. Finally, Henri in the second half of the book falls in love with Villanelle, and the two sleep together and conceive a child, yet Villanelle does not return Henri's love. Henri finishes the novel in San Servolo prison, while Villanelle raises their child in nearby Venice.

Love as truth event

It is clear that Winterson as a writer has benefited from the post-1960s freeing up of sexual expression and the increased acceptability of homosexuality, both of which gave her greater freedom as a queer female writer. But this is not the only underlying cultural shift of the past half century – love has emerged as a commodity in neoliberalism. So how can we understand the thematic of love in *The Passion* in the age of plastic sexuality[3] and individualized choices,[4] of romance as consumption in the likes of dating apps? And how is the field of the religious affected? The work of French philosopher Alain Badiou offers an entry point into understanding the ethics of love at work in Winterson's novels, as well as its religious resonances. For Badiou, love is an event, 'something that doesn't enter into the immediate order of things'.[5] He argues that 'in so far as we are given a chance of truth, a chance of being a little bit more than living individuals, pursuing our ordinary interests, this chance is always given to us through an event'.[6]

Badiou frequently investigates the event as a primarily political movement, however, his philosophy does make room for the small event of love. In his recent *In Praise of Love*, Badiou looks at love relationships in greater detail. He rails against 'safety-first'[7] approaches to love, typified by the consumerist world of online dating, which seek to guarantee love without risk. For Badiou, love 'cannot be a gift given on the basis of a complete lack of risk'.[8] Against this, Badiou argues that it is the role of philosophy as well as poetry to defend and even reinvent love.

In contrast to the 'safety-first' ethos that he sees at work in online dating, Badiou argues that the love event emerges entirely from chance: 'every singular truth has its origin in an event. Something must happen, in order for there to be something new. Even in our personal lives, there must be an encounter, there must be something which cannot be calculated, predicted or managed; there must be a break based only on chance.'[9] Badiou argues that, even for the apparently banal love story – 'So and So met his or her colleague at work'[10] – there is an element of chance that elevates the encounter to the status of 'a really radical event in life at a micro-level'. Badiou calls the event a form of 'laicized grace', an atheist version of the undeserved grace delivered by God in the Christian tradition.

From the encounter, which is strictly a random event, comes a truth that becomes universal. Love is what Badiou calls a truth-procedure, an experience which changes the subjects' relationship to truth. Yet if love stems from the chance encounter, how is truth constructed from it? For Badiou, the declaration of love marks the passage from one mode (the chance encounter) to another, the truth-procedure, which marks the beginning of life building together and the perspective of two rather than one. In a wonderful passage, Badiou states that:

> Love proves itself by permeating desire. The ritual of bodies is then the material expression of the word, it communicates the idea that the promise to re-invent life will be fulfilled, initially in terms of the body. But even in their wildest delirium, lovers know that love is there, like their bodies' guardian angel, when they wake up in the morning, when peace descends over the proof that their bodies have grasped that love has been declared.[11]

This declaration of love is important for Badiou, it marks the movement from chance to truth. As he puts it, 'to make a declaration of love is to move on from the event encounter to the construction of truth'.[12] Although this has some affinity with Foucault's discussion of confession in *The History of Sexuality* (Foucault specifically mentions 'love relations' as a site for confession), what distinguishes Badiou's declaration of love is its ability to change a situation, to reinvent two lives. And as he makes clear in *Saint Paul*, the truth-procedure has distinct aesthetic, religious and political implications.

In a quite beautiful passage, Badiou compares the truth-procedure to the 'earthen vessels' metaphor that Paul uses in the second Corinthians 4.7:

> Whoever is the subject of a truth (of love, of art, or science, or politics) knows that, in effect, he [sic] bears a treasure, that he is traversed by an infinite power. Whether or not this truth, so precarious, continues to deploy itself depends on his subjective weakness. Thus, one may justifiably say that he bears it in an earthen vessel, day after day enduring the imperative – delicacy and subtle thought – to ensure that nothing shatters it.[13]

My use of Badiou here is decidedly unBadiouan. Setting himself against deconstruction, Badiou has no truck with the undecidable, or with Levinasian-inspired politics of the other. The deconstruction of binaries, a strong theme in deconstructionist theory (and indeed Winterson as I read her), is nowhere in Badiou. In *Saint Paul*, he explicitly declares the religious content of Christianity to be a 'fable'.[14] Although the difference may appear slight, I think Winterson's reading of religion as mythic – and hence useful – is somewhat different from Badiou's Marxist materialism. Badiou states that 'I don't really like all these theological ruminations inspired by love'.[15] The broader framework of this work, in which I talk about Winterson's religious voices and the hesitation between sacred and profane, self and other, is largely incompatible with Badiou's own project of militant universality. But what *is* useful here in the analysis of *The Passion* is the way in which Badiou's philosophy of love as an event resonates with Winterson's poetics of passion and fidelity. Unlike Badiou, I *do* think that theological ruminations inspired by love are valuable. Arguably, any analysis of Winterson that focuses strictly on the secular implications (of sex, gender, historiography etc.) of her writing while neglecting the religious elements of her work presents a stunted view of a philosophically and theologically important corpus of writing.

The otherness of religion, the numinous, as Rudolph Otto termed it,[16] in my opinion forms its own truth-procedure in Winterson's novels, and it is inextricably bound up in the way Winterson imagines love.

The Passion and truth

While all of Winterson's work in some form uses love as a truth-procedure, it is her early work, *The Passion*, that is most striking. Love can be seen in Henri's passion for Napoleon, Villanelle's passion for the Queen of Spades and Henri's love for Villanelle in the second half of the novel. None of these passions end happily. At first glance, then, *The Passion* can be seen as a text about the non-arrival of love. And yet, Winterson has far more profound things to say about passion than its simple impossibility.

The necessary impossibility of passion is introduced in the novel through its great motif – that of chance. Villanelle is a card dealer in the Casino in Venice, and repeatedly likens the games of chance to that of love: 'Queen of spades you win, Ace of clubs you lose. Play again. What will you risk? Your watch? Your house? Your mistress? I like to smell the urgency on them. Even the calmest, the richest, have that smell. It's somewhere between fear and sex. Passion I suppose.'[17] It is at the casino where Villanelle witnesses a high-stakes game between a local rich man and a gambler from the Levant, in which the winner will take the other man's life. Villanelle describes the ethos of the true gambler, which she considers the rich man to be: 'the Devil's gambler keeps back something precious, something to gamble with only once in a lifetime. Behind the secret panel he keeps it, the valuable fabulous thing that nobody suspects he has.'[18] It is his life that is the man's valuable, fabulous thing, and that which he wagers and eventually loses. The two men leave the casino, never to be seen again, until one day months later a box is delivered to the casino containing a pair of hands with a roulette ball between one hand's finger and thumb and a domino piece in the other.

Immediately after recounting this story, Villanelle begins narrating the story of her love affair with the Queen of Spades: 'It was a game of chance I entered into and my heart was the wager. Such games can only be played once.'[19] As befits a love event, Villanelle meets her beloved by chance in a brief encounter at the casino, losing her in the crowd. As with gambling, Villanelle risks her life: the Queen of Spades ends up literally possessing her heart. After the chance encounter, almost immediately, the Queen of Spades begins to take over Villanelle's heart. Villanelle says: 'Memories of a single touch. How could anything so passing be pervasive? But Christ said "Follow me" and it was done.'[20] Here, Winterson explicitly compares meeting the beloved to the disciples encountering Christ, an invocation of what we can, with Badiou, call the Christ event. Meeting her beloved instantly transforms Villanelle, changing forever the coordinates of her life – even though her lover does not leave her husband and only sees Villanelle when her husband is away. For Villanelle at least, the love event sets her course, demanding an absolute fidelity.

As I have mentioned, Badiou talks about the ways in which the truth-procedure must be declared to be true. In *The Passion*, Villanelle and the Queen of Spades declare their love for one another: 'She had told me she loved me. I never doubted her word because I could feel how true it is. When she touched me I knew I was loved and with a passion I had not felt before.'[21] Love as Badiou sees it is a promise to reinvent life, starting with the physical, and the inventive power of the erotic is clear in Winterson's corpus. Villanelle herself reinvents the field of gender in her encounter with the Queen of Spades, dressing as a male soldier, then lifting her shirt and revealing her sex. Indeed, Villanelle's loving a woman 'is not the usual thing',[22] a reinvention of the romance narrative from the usual heterosexual story to one featuring a gender-fluid woman and her married female beloved.

When the Queen of Spades' husband goes away, Villanelle describes a kind of prelapsarian love affair of nine days – 'we were naked and not ashamed', a reference to Genesis 2:25 in which Adam and Eve lay in the Garden of Eden before the Fall. This image of Adam and Eve before the introduction of sin and shame into the world (in Genesis 3) is suggestive of innocence and an existential purity. Winterson imagines a brief moment of union between Villanelle and the Queen of Spades. Roland Barthes in *A Lover's Discourse* notes that we 'dream of total union: everyone says this dream is impossible, and yet it persists'.[23] While love affairs where one or both parties are married are typically represented as sordid, Villanelle's narration romanticizes the relation, ignoring possible moral ambiguities in favour of the intensity of the love event.

Eventually, however, Villanelle tires of being second-best and decides to leave Venice, so as to not be tempted to see the Queen of Spades again:

> I was angry because she had wanted me and made me want her and been afraid to accept what that meant; it meant more than brief meetings in public places and nights borrowed from someone else. Passion will work in the fields for seven years for the beloved and on being cheated work for seven more, but passion, because it is noble, will not long accept another's leftovers.[24]

Here, again, the Bible comes to stand in as a model for passionate behaviour – this time the story in Genesis of Jacob, who worked seven years to marry Rachel, only to be cheated and marry her sister Leah, and thus work another seven years to be with Rachel. This story from the Hebrew Bible illuminates that, for the Wintersonian heroine, love must be grounded in fidelity, in singularity. *The Passion* repeatedly underlines the motif of the 'fabulous thing' that must be risked – whether it be in gambling or in love.

A conversation in Winterson's later work *The PowerBook*, which shares a similar ethics to *The Passion*, shows clearly the ways in which she imagines love as a life-changing event. The narrator has the following conversation with her married paramour:

> 'I mean it's either/or.'
> 'You or him?'
> 'No. The same life or different.'
> 'I like my life.'
> 'Fine. Keep it just as it is.'
> 'But that includes you.'
> 'No. No it doesn't.'[25]

Without the reinvention of life embodied in the promise of love, a love fails. Although attracted to the forbidden in the form of married women, Winterson's lovers demand the invention of a shared life together. As Villanelle puts it, 'there is no sense in loving someone you can never wake up to except by chance'.[26] Passion demands fidelity, loyalty to the other – a movement with religious implications.

The religious love event

Although numerous critics such as Sonya Andermahr have noted the ways in which *The Passion* reinvigorates the romance narrative, there has been little interest paid to its religious resonances, which are as pervasive as any text in Winterson's canon. Villanelle is 'never tempted by God but [she] likes his trappings', going to 'churches because they were built from the heart. Hearts so full of longing that these old stones still cry out with their extasy.'[27] She 'basks' in an aesthetic experience of religion, 'taking the joy and comfort and ignoring the rest'.[28] For Villanelle, even the second-hand experience of religious passion, that of the earlier builders of churches, is enough. Here Winterson is conjuring up an individualized experience of otherness that is numinous. Religious dogma, even God himself, is jettisoned, but the sensual experience of religion – in particular, Italian Catholicism – remains a powerful force. Taking for granted the disconnection from the embedded religion of liquid modernity, Winterson's religion is an individualized form of experience that, in contrast to the love event, makes no demands on the individual, even as its forms point to an ideal of passionate behaviour.

Romance also offers a means of mediating between the transcendent and immanent. Henri notes the ways in which love is at once immanent to everyday life, but transcends it: 'Perhaps all romance is like that; not a contract between equal parties but an explosion of dreams and desires that can find no outlet in everyday life.'[29] The love event is notable for the ways in which it creatively reinvents life. For Badiou, as with the Pauline letters, the formal structure of the love event has political implications. Yet we can also see within Winterson's love events the structure of a relation to the ineffable – a risky, uncertain, life-changing relation that demands a certain fidelity, even as circumstances show the impossibility of completion. The 'valuable, fabulous thing' that the gambler risks is life itself, which is worth risking for the experience of transcending the banality of the everyday.

Winterson's response to the individualized, liquid modern world, after the death of God, is to proffer passion as a transcendental value. As literary critic Michelle Denby puts it:

> *The Passion*'s title, with its central allusion to the 'Passion narratives', the account in the canonical Gospels of Christ's mental and physical suffering prior to and during the crucifixion, introduces its key definition of passion as both suffering and pleasure. Christ's 'Agony', counterbalanced by the pleasure of offering eternal life, which reappears in the symbiosis of suffering and freedom in mystical writing, mirrors the protagonists' own experience of passion.[30]

Just like Christians experience fidelity to the event of Christ on the cross, only fidelity to the love event provides a world-shaping orientation, a solidity to the liquidity of a modernity without sure boundaries anywhere else. Against the endless array of choices, Winterson offers a kind of fatalism – 'love will not be commanded'.[31]

Philosopher of religion John Caputo has discussed the event. Caputo uses a Deleuzian rather than Badiouian take, yet his work has strong resonances with my analysis of Winterson's love events. Caputo argues that events are excessive, that 'they overtake us and outstrip the reach of the subject or the ego'.[32] He suggests that 'an event is an irruption, an excess, an overflow, a gift beyond economy, which tears open the closed circles of economics'.[33] Caputo argues that names, most especially the name of God, contain events, but the event is uncontainable. The name of God '*harbors* an event',[34] but it is elusive and unpredictable, swelling within the name but not reducible to it. As Deleuze puts it, 'to the extent that events are actualized within us, they wait for us and invite us in. They signal us'.[35]

For Winterson, the name of God is such an event. What swell within the name, within the warm walls of the church, are 'hearts full of longing'. When speaking of the desire heterosexual men feel for women, Henri notes that he is using 'Bible words again', that passion turns men into 'something holy'.[36] Passion swells within the name, whether it be for God, the Bible, a political leader or for the beloved. In the end, for Winterson, what matters is that the love event is released, that the full weight of desire is ushered into being, however briefly; Henri describes passion as fireworks: 'while the fireworks last the sky is a different colour'.[37] Passion is creative, spectacular, but it comes with an ethical demand for fidelity, for the reinvention of a life.

Yet, as an event, the seeds of catastrophe may also swell within the name. Henri's love for Napoleon sees him follow the Emperor to bloody disaster: 2,000 dead men drowned in an attempted invasion of England. Villanelle's love for the Queen of Spades means she loses her heart, while Henri's love for Villanelle sees him imprisoned for murdering her ex-husband. Henri is single-minded in his determination to only accept the beloved, choosing to remain in the San Servelo prison rather than accept Villanelle's half-hearted, 'brotherly, incestuous' love.[38] He says: 'I say I'm in love with her, what does that mean? It means I review my future and my past in the light of this feeling. It is as though I wrote in a foreign language that I am suddenly able to read. Wordlessly she explains me to myself; like genius she is ignorant of what she does.'[39] Henri disparages the calculating, lukewarm embrace of passion-free love. Although Villanelle notes that 'the one who took your heart wields final power',[40] for Henri the fidelity he feels is not precisely to Villanelle in herself – he will not leave the prison when she offers to break him out – because she will not love him in the way he wishes.

Instead, Henri's allegiance is to the love event in itself. The love event must be accepted in its entirety, with a kind of fatalism as to the consequences – otherwise, for Winterson, it is not a love event at all. Henri thus chooses to stay in prison, and his mind disintegrates into madness, a warning of the double-edged nature of love, which as Badiou reminds us, 'is not necessarily any more peaceful than revolutionary politics'.[41] Just as Napoleon led thousands of Frenchmen to their deaths, Henri's love for Villanelle leads him to insanity. Caputo says that 'the excess of the event is not necessarily good news', for 'every promise is also a threat, and the event to come can be either for better or for worse'.[42] Nevertheless, it is clear from *The Passion* that Winterson fatalistically embraces the consequences of the event, in an embrace of the excessive. Indeed, this desire for the excess of the event is endorsed by Henri, who states that 'we fear passion and laugh at too much love and those who love too much. And still we long to feel.'[43]

What might it mean for Henri to 'long to feel'? In the first section of the novel, Henri's passion is a platonic desire for Napoleon, a political passion founded on personal charisma: 'He was in love with himself and France joined in.'[44] Henri disparages 'lukewarm' passion, looking for the intensity of the love event instead. This too is linked to the religious, although there is an atheistic (or at least agnostic) interest here, as when Henri states: 'I'm not interested in the still small voice. Surely a god can meet passion with passion?'[45] Here we see Winterson's transformations of binaries, the fluid movement between differing spheres – if religious passion comes to stand in for romantic passion (as in the reference to Jacob's passion for Rachel), the religious here needs the intensity of romantic devotion. Religion is a kind of romance in *The Passion*, just as romance is a kind of religion.

Conclusion

Winterson's narrativizing of love emerges from the epistemological background of what sociologist Zygmunt Bauman has called liquid modernity, the increasing fluidity of life biographies in the twentieth and twenty-first centuries.[46] But Winterson is at pains to distinguish her writing from the contemporary taxonomical cataloguing of what feminist theorist Wendy Brown calls 'ascriptive identities' – selves marked by features like sex, gender, race and sexuality.[47] In *Art Objects*, Winterson explicitly takes issue with simple identity politics that neatly conflate her art with her lesbianism. She argues instead for the universalist emotional experience that emerges from literature: 'Literature, whether made by heterosexuals or homosexuals, whether to do with lives gay or straight, packs in it supplies of energy and emotion that all of us need.'[48] The function of literature, indeed all art, for Winterson is the 'realisation of complex emotion'[49] tied to important life events and the examination of taboos. Art offers a defamiliarization of the world, helping the reader to 're-evaluate what things matter, what things we take for granted'.[50] While Winterson considers the role of art as universal, innate even, she argues that, in gendering art, we look to 'find ways to contain and [reduce the] fascinating fear'[51] that art provokes – that is to say, we seek to contain the uncontainable, the event.

In other words, Winterson sees the role of the artist being to provoke her audience with truth. Although many of her texts deal with sexual relationships between women – which many would call lesbian – her work functions in a universalizing mode. Confession, which as Foucault notes in the first volume of *The History of Sexuality*, is a dominant technique of modernity, is indeed everywhere in Winterson. Instead, although Foucault's 'incitement to discourse' in narrating sexuality is not flouted (how could it be?),[52] Winterson is at pains to narrativize relationships as specificities, as intense events that are singular in the connection they produce. Yet the modern drive to connect this confession with identity – sexuality as the 'truth' of a person – is thwarted by Winterson. With bisexual characters in numerous books (e.g. *The Passion, Written on the Body, Gut Symmetries* and *The PowerBook*), Winterson refuses the idea that it is mere gender that determines the truth of a love event. The experiment of obscuring the narrator of *Written on the Body*, furthermore, is an attempt to write a love story without sexual categorization – the romantic relationship cannot be easily read as heterosexual or homosexual. Where sociologist Anthony Giddens noted that more and more relationships over the course of the twentieth century have been 'pure relationships',[53] freed of the demands of survival or reproduction, Winterson takes this movement one step further and purifies the relationship of gendered and sexual norms. The love event is thus, formally, a universally available event. Similarly, Winterson's work underlines the universal nature of the religious event, of the intrusion of the sacred into the ordinary.

As an event, love promises a 'little bit more' than the ordinary turn of events, just as the event of the sacred does. Sociologist of religion Mircea Eliade terms the intrusion of the sacred into the profane a hierophany. I have elsewhere discussed how contemporary fiction (in particular, 'unreal' fiction) may be regarded as a second-hand hierophany.[54] Eliade defines the term hierophany as the interruption of the everyday, when '*something sacred shows itself to us*'.[55] Arguably as an ir/religious mystic, Winterson's love events can be seen as functioning as a hierophany.

Winterson's work shows faith in the impossible, in the unconditional. Caputo talks about a 'sacred anarchy', 'bodies raised from the dead, of Jesus walking on water or passing through solid walls, of miracles, healings and angelic visitations [...] a world turned inside out and upside down by divine power'.[56] What is the magical world of *The Passion* if not a sacred anarchy, a 'poetics of the impossible' as Caputo terms it? Villanelle walks on water with her webbed feet (normally, according to her, only possessed by the male boatman of Venice); the priest Patrick can see for miles; Napoleon's horse is tended to by Domino, a midget from a circus; and, of course, there is Villanelle's play with gender. Numerous critics have seen this anarchic world of *The Passion* as a kind of postmodern play with narrative, a historiographic metafiction that undercuts traditional notions of history, with Napoleon's campaigns narrated by a lowly kitchen hand. While this has a certain validity, arguably it ignores Winterson's ambivalence about postmodernism, which is manifest both in her ethics of the love event and in her representation of religion, as well as the way she narrates her own work as a kind of modernist practice in *Art Objects*.

Although Winterson cannot escape the historical time period in which she is writing, and the ways in which liquid, postmodern capitalism inflects her work – her idiosyncratic individuals have a kind of self-determined sovereignty typical of the neoliberal subject – arguably what is distinctive about *The Passion* is the ways in which it manifests what Badiou calls a 'passion for the Real'.[57] Badiou deploys the term 'the Real' in all its Lacanian implications of the unpresentable, the impossible to symbolize, but we should also run together the Real with the sublime, the ineffable, the impossible. Love, whose model is religious love, is sublime in Winterson's work, and transforms the field of representation profoundly. The event is something miraculous, something unforeseen that makes life worth living. Sitting on the boundary between religious and irreligious, Winterson continually collapses the opposition between transcendent and immanent.

4

Sexing the Cherry and the Monstrous Maternal

It is clear from works like *The Passion* and *Written on the Body* that Winterson is interested in idealized forms of romantic love. Yet lurking behind it is a persistent interest in mothers, in the maternal. We see this in the 'cover version' of Winterson's life in *Oranges Are Not the Only Fruit*, of course, not to mention the rawer memoir story of *Why Be Happy When You Could Be Normal?*, but arguably the most interesting take on motherhood in Winterson's corpus is to be found in *Sexing the Cherry*, where much of the book is written from the perspective of a mother – and a giant mother at that. In this chapter, I shall discuss Winterson's carnivalesque take on the monstrous maternal in the novel. The monster, as Jeffrey Jerome Cohen once wrote in *Monster Theory*, is the harbinger of a category crisis, dwelling at the gates of difference, less a character than a sign to be read.[1] There are distinctly gendered dimensions to monstrosity because, as Barbara Creed has argued, 'when woman is represented as monstrous it is almost always in relation to her mothering and reproductive functions'.[2] Furthermore, monstrous mothers confuse and confound hegemonic Christian ideas of motherhood as contained and controllable. In contrast, Winterson's monstrous mother, I argue, in all her complicated ambivalent monstrosity, draws our attention to the sacred in the ways that it problematizes religiously produced hierarchies of bodies.

Sexing the Cherry

Sexing the Cherry, like *The Passion*, is a novel primarily written from the perspective of two characters – Dog Woman, and her son Jordan – who live in London during the time of Charles II. Dog Woman is a giant, monstrous and dirty, while Jordan is a cross-dressing adventurer who sails the world and brings the first pineapple to England. Towards the end of the novel, the perspective shifts to another pair – one Nicholas Jordan, a dreamy Navy cadet, and an unnamed woman protesting against a polluting factory – and then back again. Rather than representing a shift from a fantastic narrative to a realist story, the abrupt changes in point of view seem to suggest a troubling of the boundary between real and unreal, history and imagination. As literary critics Helena Grice and Tim Woods put it, '*Sexing the Cherry* is about the insertion of fantasy into what is taken to be reality, or history, and the supposed fixed opposition of these two categories.'[3] Needless to say, these are typically Wintersonian concerns of the early 1990s, when her writing more strongly evidenced a postmodern concern with historiographic metafiction than in later works.[4]

The monstrous maternal

Andermahr notes the similarities between *Sexing the Cherry* and Mikhail Bakhtin's theories of the carnivalesque, a quotidian destabilization, suspension or inversion of ruling binaries. Both Dog Woman and Jordan disturb the boundaries between male and female, straight and queer, human and monster. In particular, Dog Woman challenges normative ideas of what it means to be female and a mother. She is described as hideous: 'How hideous am I? My nose is flat, my eyebrows are heavy. I have only a few teeth and those are a poor show, being black and broken. I had smallpox when I was a girl and the caves in my face are home enough for fleas.'[5] The Dog Woman's monstrosity is sexually coded – she bites off a man's penis when giving fellatio, and swallows a man into her vagina while having sex with him. Susana Onega suggests that 'the Dog Woman's monstrosity is located in her lower half and is associated with her sexual power'.[6] This is arguably a queer monstrosity, for as Sonya Andermahr has noted, 'the question of Dog Woman's sexuality is an interesting one: putatively heterosexual, she resists normative categorisation'.[7] Dog Woman is not easily or only heterosexual, despite her encounters with men. Indeed, there is a distinct bawdiness to Dog Woman, for as Jane Haslett has argued, 'uncontrollable, flowing, enormous, ugly, violent, tender, loving, energetic, smelly, noisy, rough, dirty, Dog Woman's body is everything the female body is *not* supposed to be'[8] – an excess that many contemporary writers would take to be queer.

If Dog Woman's body is not normatively female, then what exactly is it? The French/Bulgarian psychoanalyst and literary theorist Julia Kristeva has written famously about what she calls the *abject*, which may illuminate some aspects of Winterson's monstrous imaginings. In *Powers of Horror*, Kristeva writes about the ways in which certain physical features of the body come to be experienced as disgusting and expelled, and even threaten the formation of the self and its place in the world. She asks, 'why does *corporeal waste*, menstrual blood and excrement, or everything that is assimilated to them, from nail-parings to decay, represent – like a metaphor that would have become incarnate – the objective frailty of symbolic order?'[9] Kristeva notes the ways in which 'a large number of rituals and discourses involved in making up the sacred' are concerned with 'defilement'.[10] She particularly notes the presence of these prohibitions in such formations as Jewish dietary laws, which are clearly arbitrary between the clean and the unclean. Kristeva suggests that behind the surface fear of defilement by abject objects (we might give the example of pork, unclean to both Muslims and Jews) we might find the more archaic taboos of death and incest.

What is clear in *Sexing the Cherry* is that Dog Woman's body is indeed an abject one. One of the ways by which cultural monstrosity emerges is through a lack of measure, a lack of control. Size in itself can become monstrous if it is deemed excessive. As Susan Stewart put it in her ground-breaking *On Longing*, 'the gigantic represents infinity, exteriority, the public, and the overly natural'.[11] We should note the excess within this statement, the 'overly' natural, the ways in which our view of 'nature' comes with implicit measurements. Dog Woman is depicted as being huge – as literary critic Sara Martin notes, 'her gross physicality is expressed in terms that border on the surrealist as, for instance, in the scene in which she catapults a circus elephant out of sight with a thrust of her heavy body'[12] – and, given the graphic sex scene in which her vagina swallows a man, grotesquely sexual, that is to say, abject. Stewart notes that 'we are enveloped by the gigantic, surrounded by it, enclosed within its shadow'.[13] Dog Woman's body is an abject body that presents a clear threat to the Puritans around her who fear excess of any kind, from sex to the theatre to Dog Woman herself.

Indeed, Dog Woman's abject qualities are signalled through repeated attention to her body, which is characterized as dirty and smelly. She 'hate[s] to wash, for it exposes the skin to contamination'.[14] Instead, she 'follow[s] the habit of King James, who only ever washed his fingertips and yet was pure in heart enough to give us the Bible in good English'.[15] Onega notes that Dog Woman's dirtiness makes her literally an Earth Mother. 'Her love for Jordan and her mountainous shape clearly identify her with the earth, with its connotations of maternity, cyclical renewal and cosmic regeneration.'[16] Onega notes that Dog Woman finds Jordan in the earth, 'so caked in mud I could have baked him like a hedgehog'.[17]

The maternal and the divine

Having followed feminist criticism of *Sexing the Cherry* along a more or less conventional path in reading the maternal as monstrous, I would now like to extend that discussion in examining the religious connotations of maternity. In doing so, I will turn again to Kristeva; however, this will take in some of her more obscure work on belief and gender. In her 1987 work *In The Beginning Was Love*, Kristeva analyses religion – primarily Christianity – through a psychoanalytic lens. She equates the maternal with the pre-linguistic, noting the gendered qualities of Plato's *chora*, 'prior to the One, to the father, and even to the syllable, metaphorically suggesting something nourishing and maternal'.[18] For Kristeva, union with the mother comes first, before culture and language. She notes that, in reading about mystic experiences, she 'felt that faith could be described, perhaps rather simplistically, as what can only be called a primary identification with a loving and protective agency'.[19] Faith can be thought of as a kind of substitution for the maternal, a 'fusion with the Other that is no longer substantial and maternal but symbolic and paternal'.[20]

Kristeva discusses the work of St Augustine, who compares Christian faith to an infant's feeding from its mother. For Kristeva, this suggests that faith is a movement from the materiality of the mother's body to the world of signs. She says, 'what we have here is a fusion with a breast that is, to be sure, succoring, nourishing, loving, and protective, but transposed from the mother's body to an invisible agency located in another world'.[21] She notes that 'the benefits of the new relationship of dependency are entirely of an imaginary order, in the realm of signs'.[22] And yet, while this easily could be seen as straightforwardly psychoanalytic insight into the maturation of the subject (the movement from mother to the linguistic father is, after all, thematized in Lacan's gloss on the Oedipus complex), Kristeva is suggesting that this transference still remains in the realm of what she calls the semiotic. She argues:

> [T]his is perhaps what Christianity celebrates in divine love. God was the first to love you; God is love: these apothegms reassure the believer of God's permanent generosity and grace. He is given a gift of love without any immediate requirement of merit [...] This fusion with God, which [...] is more semiotic than symbolic, repairs the wounds of Narcissus, which are scarcely hidden by the triumphs and failures of our desires and enmities.[23]

Divine love is therefore a kind of unacknowledged maternal love in this sense, even as God is described in paternal terms. Kristeva thus sees the role of faith in remarkably positive terms, especially given the suspicion towards faith of many psychoanalysts from Freud onwards.[24]

Kristeva moves on to discussing mothers, and unsurprisingly this discussion centres on the role of the Virgin Mary in Christianity. She says: 'a virgin mother? We want our mothers to be virgins, so that we can love them better or allow ourselves to be loved by them without fear of a rival.'[25] She suggests that Christianity's union of father and son was achieved by reducing the weight of the father's symbolic authority through the removal of procreative sexuality. The believer 'protects itself against a fantasy that is too much for any child to bear: that of being supernumerary, excluded from the act of pleasure that is the origin of its existence'.[26] Instead, 'Christianity [...] avoids the whole question of procreation.'[27] In this sense, for Kristeva, Christianity avoids the Oedipus complex.[28]

We can see this functioning in an interesting fashion in *Sexing the Cherry*. Dog Woman finds Jordan by the side of the Thames, in a scene that is explicitly compared to the story of Moses in Exodus. Although she is coded as monstrous, and specifically as a sexual kind of monstrous, Dog Woman in this sense remains a virgin mother –

sex is removed from the scene of Jordan's procreation. As she puts it, 'I would have liked to pour out a child from my body but you have to have a man for that and there's no man who's a match for me.'[29] Jordan takes his name from the sacred river in Israel which is the site of numerous episodes in the Bible. As Dog Woman tells it:

> I call him Jordan and it will do. He has no other name before or after. What was there to call him, fished as he was from the stinking Thames? A child can't be called Thames, no and not Nile either, for all his likeness to Moses. But I wanted to give him a river name, a name not bound to anything, just as the waters aren't bound to anything.[30]

Here Winterson shows a thematic interest in waters, in literal fluidity, as a metaphor for the slippery nature of identity – a slipperiness that she equates with religious narrative as much as the breaking of sex and gender norms.

Winterson compares Jordan to the story of Moses in Exodus in the Hebrew Bible, in which the Pharaoh of Egypt tells the Israelites to discard their male babies in the Nile river. Moses' mother puts him in a basket, which is found by Pharaoh's daughter, who ends up raising Moses as an Egyptian prince. The story then is one of adoption, a frequent motif in the Winterson corpus, and unsurprising given Winterson's own adoption. Furthermore, many Christians have seen the story of Moses, a foundling, as a typological foreshadowing of Christ's life, with Moses' imperilled young life a kind of mirroring of the mythical origins of Christ in the Book of Matthew. Both spent their childhoods in Egypt, for as Matthew 2:14 puts it: 'So he [Jesus' father Joseph] got up, took the child and his mother during the night and left for Egypt, where he stayed until the death of Herod. And so was fulfilled what the Lord had said through the prophet: "Out of Egypt I called my son."'[31] So, for Jordan to be compared to Moses is a theologically rich – one might even say pregnant – move on

Winterson's part, for it situates Jordan in reference to both Moses and Christ, and Dog Woman as recalling both Pharaoh's daughter and the Virgin Mary.

Although Winterson in so many ways in her work has refigured the sexual economy of Christianity, here the function of the mother remains traditionally chaste. Dog Woman says, 'I am too huge for love. No one, male or female, has ever dared to approach me. They are afraid to scale mountains.'[32] The gigantic, as Stewart has said, is an overly natural phenomenon, and we see this here in Dog Woman's correlation between her size and her ability to be loved. This is linked to religious imaginaries of love, for Dog Woman notes that 'I wonder about love because the parson says that only God can truly love us and the rest is lust and selfishness.'[33] And yet, at the same time, Dog Woman has seen the arousal of her fellow church-goers and 'noticed a bulge here and there where all should be quiet and God-like'.[34] In the end, however, it is maternal love that Dog Woman finds to be truest, in which 'the love I've known has come from my dogs, who care nothing for how I look, and from Jordan, who says that though I am as wide and muddy as the river that is his namesake, so am I too his kin'.[35] In the end, therefore, Dog Woman's monstrosity becomes symbolically intertwined with the sacred and with maternal love.

So, despite her sexual coding as an excessively embodied queerness at times, Dog Woman does not actually have sex for pleasure or particularly experience desire – her desire is more often articulated for her son. She says, 'I know what love sounds like because I have heard it through the wall, but I do not know what it feels like.'[36] She has a peculiar kind of innocence about sex in some ways, thinking that penises grow back when bitten off. Dog Woman is a mother but not a lover, an unlikely Virgin Mary figure of the monstrous maternal.

In order to understand Dog Woman's monstrous maternity as specifically religious, we must return again to the archetypal mother of Western civilization – the Virgin Mary. Of course, Kristeva is far from the only feminist theorist to have contributed to modern thought about the Virgin Mary. Marcella Althaus-Reid has talked about the way in which the Virgin Mary is glossed in misogynistic terms in the Christian tradition. She says, 'Christian issues of humility and submission to God come from that premise: the ejaculatory movement of the Word of God requires an immobile receptacle, such as the Virgin Mary.'[37] For Althaus-Reid, the Virgin Mary is defined by her passivity. As feminist theologian Elizabeth Johnson has noted too in her study of the Virgin Mary *Truly Our Sister*, the 'strong emphasis on Mary's obedience, virginity, and primary importance as a mother shaped a religious symbol that satisfied the needs of a monastic or ecclesiastical male psyche more adequately than it served women's spiritual or social capabilities'.[38]

But this does not need to be the only way to understand the Virgin Mary, as Althaus-Reid and Johnson make clear in very different ways. We can see a refiguring of the monstrous virgin maternal in Winterson, too. Literary critic Jeffrey Roessner notes the significance of the metaphor of grafting in *Sexing the Cherry*, which suggests to him that Winterson is interested in hybrid identities and practices. If we look at her from another angle to the traditional view of Christianity, Mary can be seen as a hybrid of opposites – virgin and mother – a grafting together of disparate and impossibly coexisting elements. Mary thus becomes a monster, whose body is overdetermined with conflicting meanings about sex, gender and bodies. What might be found there, then? Althaus-Reid has questioned the presumed heterosexuality of Mary, asking, 'why not Mary the Queer of Heaven? The fact that nothing is known of Mary or God's sexual identity liberates them; nothing is fixed.'[39] Instead, Althaus-Reid talks of 'indecenting Mary',[40] which means freeing Mary from the rigid sex, gender and sexuality matrix of Christianity.

In grafting together opposites, then, Winterson collapses binaries and forms a third way, something as novel and provocative as anything Althaus-Reid can imagine. Both Dog Woman's monstrous maternity and the cross-dressing adventurer Jordan show a disdain for binaries, especially those of the Puritan establishment of the novel's setting. Dog Woman is an indecent woman, one who attracts disgust and disdain for her body. We can therefore see a provocative attention to remaking the Christian hierarchy of bodies and desires, resuscitating old stereotypes of virginal mothers into new, wilder and more compelling takes on embodied maternity.

What is unusual about Winterson's abject maternity in *Sexing the Cherry* is the way in which it shows Dog Woman as having an agency. She may be monstrous, but she is far from pitiable, and definitely far from passive. For instance, when Jordan lays dying of the plague, she threatens her witch friend in a fit of 'maternal rage'. Jordan notes that this mother is a 'fantasist, a liar and a murderer', but that he still loves her. Here once again we see Winterson problematizing boundaries, between queer and straight, mother and monster, secular and sacred.

It is not simply in Dog Woman's story that we find *Sexing the Cherry* interrogating the Christian hierarchy of bodies. Jordan cross-dresses in the novel, finding sanctuary in living as a woman for a time. He says:

> In my petticoats I was a traveller in a foreign country [...] I watched women flirting with men, pleasing men, doing business with men, and then I watched them collapse with laughter, sharing the joke, while the men, all unknowing, felt themselves master of the situation and went off to brag in bar-rooms and preach from the pulpits the folly of the weaker sex.[41]

Important here is the way in which pulpits are associated with maleness, with patriarchy, with an official narrative that suppresses women's knowledge. As a result, the Puritan religion is literally a joke to women, and it is Jordan's movement between genders that makes possible the excavation of this knowledge. Language itself, which is associated with the paternal role of the divine father, becomes usurped by a marginal knowledge discovered by the movement from male to female, powerful to powerless. Interestingly, Jordan's gender transgression is *not* depicted as abject or pathological, as is usual for representations of gender diversity.

Exposing hypocrisy

One of the most interesting themes of *Sexing the Cherry* is the hypocrisy of the Puritan religious establishment, which touches on broader Wintersonian themes of the insufficiency of established religions for expressing passion authentically. Roessner notes that 'Winterson represents the [Puritan] Revolution as a clear battle between King Charles I – the servant of God who goes with dignity to his execution – and the sexually repressed and hypocritical Puritans'.[42] As Dog Woman puts it, Puritans 'hated everything that was grand and fine and full of life'.[43] Instead, Dog Woman would 'rather lives with sins of excess than sins of denial'.[44] She states that: 'The Puritans, who wanted a rule of saints on earth and no king but Jesus, forgot that we are born into flesh and in flesh must remain. Their women bind their breasts and cook plain food without salt, and the men are so afraid of their member uprising that they keep it strapped between their legs in bandages.'[45] Here we see Winterson's preference for Catholicism emerging once again – just as we see a qualified endorsement of Catholic sensuality in *The Passion* and *Art & Lies*. Puritanism in *Sexing the Cherry* is an intensified form of the kind of Protestantism that Winterson is deeply suspicious of, a denial of the self and the myriad forms of pleasure that Winterson's work evokes in positive terms (sexuality, food, art, music). Where *Oranges* maintains an ambivalence towards the Protestantism of Winterson's childhood, seeing community and connection to God there, too, *Sexing the Cherry* puts forth an unequivocal denunciation of Puritanism.

We can see this in Dog Woman's murderous rage against Puritans, which is a key facet of her monstrous maternal characterization. She murders the hypocritical Puritans Pastor Scrogg and her neighbour Firebrace, in a brothel as they have a *ménage à trois* with a sex worker. There is an element of justice to this, as Pastor Scrogg's wife thanks Heaven for her good fortune. Dog Woman comes as an avenging executioner, another aspect of her Earth Mother characterization. We can therefore see Dog Woman's murders as embodying a female rage at patriarchy, especially the stifling Puritan masculinity that threatens the women around her. Dog Woman's sympathies are with other similarly ugly, monstrous women, and outcasts like prostitutes. While it is possible to see this as Christ-like – after all, Jesus did associate with the outcasts of society himself and expose the hypocrisy of the religious establishment – it is a queer, feminist interest in alterity that is being put forth here, and one that is distinctly maternal. As Paulina Palmer has put it, Winterson 'challenges phallocentric definitions of femininity',[46] both herself as an author and in the way she writes her female characters.

One could easily read Dog Woman's disdain for the Puritans as an atheist critique of organized religion and its many excesses. This would be one, perfectly valid, way of reading *Sexing the Cherry*; however, I would like to trouble the border between belief and unbelief in suggesting that Dog Woman's monstrosity and queer maternal rage may have some spiritual value. In fighting the Puritans, Dog Woman arguably is searching for a better, less hypocritical form of religion rather than simply being an atheistic dismissal. She sees in the older Catholic religion of England a more truthful and meaningful religion.

We can therefore see in *Sexing the Cherry* the ways in which Winterson is interested in grafting together different elements to create new forms. Where some critics have seen this primarily in terms of gender and sexuality, arguably it is also a religious grafting that sees the sacred expressed *through* those gendered and sexual forms. The ambivalent monstrous maternal points us towards Kristeva's semiotic union with the mother in ways that signal towards the sacred.

5

Written on the Body and the Negative Theology Tradition

In this chapter, I shall read Winterson's *Written on the Body* as a novelistic body that lets loose gendered, sexual and religious meanings, silences and ambivalences. Many of these stem from the prime conceit of the novel: the narrator of *Written on the Body* as the book's back cover reveals is 'gender undeclared'.[1] Despite this explicit gambit, 'many critics', as literary critic Brian Finney argues, 'choose to assume the narrator is a thinly disguised lesbian lover [...] they promptly foreclose a text that Winterson has deliberately left open'.[2] Instead, I wish to leave the text open, examining its relation to sex and gender variance without being tied to determinate readings.

By opening up the field of ambiguity, and in its alliance of gender and sexuality with the sacred, *Written on the Body* comes close to what Argentinian theologian Marcella Althaus-Reid has called an 'indecent theology'.[3] In *The Queer God*, Althaus-Reid argues that 'belief systems are organized around people's bodies, and people's bodies in relationships, and in sexual relationships'.[4] She argues that religious belief is inextricably linked to sexual, gendered, raced and classed ideologies that are mediated through the body. The kinds of bodies in the Christian imaginary, most especially that of God 'himself', are organized normatively, produced as discursive power along the lines of heterosexist, racist, misogynistic and imperialist thought. As well as the idealized bodies of the spiritual, aberrant bodies are produced which become formally constituted outside the purvey of theology, and indeed outside religion and religious communities in general (or, less formally, relegated unacknowledged inside the closet). To counter this, Althaus-Reid centres her analysis on the experiences of these abject bodies more usually excluded from theological consideration – drag queens, poor women, sex workers, gays and lesbians, gender variant people, BDSM practitioners etc.

Althaus-Reid is still indebted to a cataphatic project of representation, albeit of an unorthodox kind, yet other responses to the limited imaginary of Christianity have long been a part of theological discussion. Negative theology, or apophatic (that which 'unsays' or 'says away') thought, addresses the incompleteness of the language used to describe the divine in a different way. Negative theology, as the name suggests, denies that God can be described positively, even up to the name 'God' itself, for to do so is a form of idolatry. As Meister Eckhart admonishes, 'be silent and do not chatter about God, for when you chatter about him, you are telling lies and sinning'.[5] It is this that will allow us to make sense of the ways in which *Written on the Body* obscures the body of its narrator, and the theological implications of this gesture.

Negation

Negative theology has long been a form of Christian theological discourse. Its prominent writers have included Nicholas of Cusa, Meister Eckhart and Pseudo-Dionysius. More recently, negative theology has been a matter of interest for deconstructively minded philosophers,[6] theologians[7] and literary theorists.[8] The basic premise of negative theology is that the transcendent cannot be described directly by language. Since the transcendent, by definition, is not of this earth it cannot be described within any definition of the sacred formed by earthly experience. God, therefore, only can be described negatively by what 'he' is *not*. Apophatic language therefore suggests that earthly concepts are inadequate to the task of describing or producing the sacred, except negatively. Characteristic of this is fifteenth-century mystic Nicholas of Cusa who argues that 'the language of negation is so necessary to the theology of affirmation that without it God would not be worshiped as the infinite God but as creature; and such worship is idolatry, for it gives to an image that which belongs only to truth itself'.[9] In other words, to situate God as an embodied creature is to always-already create an idol.

Yet, despite this position, as Catherine Keller argues, apophatic theology has found it harder to negate the image of God as male than Being itself. She says: 'this radicality did not in its traditional texts greatly disturb the masculinity of the infinite. If beyond all finite attributions he transcended His gender, His gender exercised its own transcendence, its own negation of any negation of masculinity (O Lord!)'.[10] So, even after all the negations of negative theology, male writers have struggled to discard the normatively male body. Keller points out that the female body itself has been the 'not quite speakable sex'.[11] But Winterson appears to go even further, into what Keller would call a 'queer fold' of feminist unsaying, with a body with no discernible sex.

Other recent engagements with negative theology have been similarly silent on the subject of sex and gender. In the deconstructive iterations of negative theology, apophatic thought can be said to be about deconstructing presence – very much the intellectual project of the early Jacques Derrida. Like Derrida's infamous *différance*, the God of negative theologians is often neither presence nor absence. Nicholas of Cusa, for instance, suggests that 'if God were to be understood, then he would be understood to not be an other'.[12] In other words, God is not-other because he cannot be figured out – neither 'something' nor 'other than something'. And yet, as Derrida points out in 'How to Avoid Speaking', his most direct encounter with apophatic theology, '"negative theology" seems to reserve, beyond all positive predication, beyond all negation, even Being, some hyperessentially, a being beyond Being'.[13] Yet despite his wish to evade such hidden metaphysics of presence, Derrida remains silent on the subject of sex and negative theology. In order to bring out *Written on the Body*'s gender ambiguity as a spiritual principle, we will have to look elsewhere for intellectual support.

Gender ambiguities

Sexual difference, as numerous feminist and queer writers have noted, is a compulsory binaristic regime in Anglophonic countries.[14] People are gendered as *either* male or female, their bodies sexed as one or the other. These signs and their histories are stabilized as fixed and natural through repeated citation.[15] Institutions are organized around a mutually exclusive sex binary (male *or* female), a biopolitical movement that divides the human race into two sexes from before birth[16] to death. From birth certificates to driver's licences to passports and death certificates, almost all forms of identification contain a demarcation between male and female. This has a widespread social effect, since, as trans-theorist Viviane Namaste points out, 'the practical work of institutions is textually organized around documents',[17] working to distribute bodies in space according to sex (in the form of often mutually exclusive sex-designated toilets, prisons, schools, hospitals, government services, homeless shelters etc.).

Yet there are, of course, exceptions which problematize easy categorization in these regimes. Intersex is a broad term used to describe bodies that are 'naturally' sexed outside of the bounds of normatively male and female, 'those where an individual's genitalia appears "ambiguous" or where the genitalia appearance does not "match" the chromosomal configuration'.[18] Transsexual is a term used to describe people whose sexed bodies and gender presentations are another sex from that they were assigned at birth (that is, transsexual people are presumed to have 'crossed' from one sex to the other). And transgender is a broader term used to describe transsexual men and women, genderqueers, drag kings and queens, and other gender-variant people. All of these provide epistemological challenges to the naturalization process of the sex/gender regime, yet they do not change the pervasive and compulsory element of sexual difference. Although many people (i.e. genderqueers/non-binary and some intersexed people) may live and *identify* as a third gender, an identification which has a certain declamatory force of its own, they nevertheless do not step outside the compulsory regimes that constitute the sexed body as an object of legal, social and political interest – to do so is a cultural impossibility in most parts of the world.[19] One can be received as an unorthodoxly sexed or gendered man or woman, or a perverted or failed man or woman, but not as a person who is not one of the two. Further, one cannot do without a legal sex and its attendant institutional distribution of bodies in space and rights (who can marry who, for instance).

Therefore, it is an impossible cultural position that the narrator of *Written on the Body* stakes out, for they are, as the book's back cover reveals, 'gender undeclared'. The self-narrating character goes to some lengths to obscure their sex and gender, talking in the first person and avoiding personal pronouns and self-description as male or female altogether. Other characters use second-person pronouns ('you') and gender-neutral descriptions. For instance, the narrator's lover Louise says, 'when I saw you two years ago I thought you were the most beautiful creature male or female I had ever seen.'[20] In one passage, Winterson shifts to a third-person narrator, imagining a play in which the narrator is referred to only as 'the lover' in contrast to 'naked woman.'[21] Here, the narrator's lack of sex is particularly noticeable in comparison to the other character, whose 'womanness' is emphasized in its nudity, a nudity that 'the lover' lacks. Instead, the sexed body of the narrator remains unknowable. 'I like to keep my body rolled up away from prying eyes. Never unfold too much, tell the whole story.'[22]

Indeed, it is arguable that, in this obscuration of the sexed body and gendered overdetermination, the narrator of *Written on the Body* has a proximity to gender variant populations (transgender, intersex, butch and genderqueer). Simply because gender *is* compulsorily declared and institutionally produced, the narrator plays with gender in a manner that is particularly suggestive of those sex/gender variances which are either fluid, indeterminate or create a mismatch in sex/gender regimes between the sexed body and normative gender presentation that is presumed to follow. By deferring a final self-description, the narrator 'decides not to decide', as Myfanwy McDonald evocatively characterizes non-surgical forms of gender identity.[23] Here, newer forms of gender diversity join up with older poetic takes on androgyny and hermaphroditism.

Of course, positioning the narrator as *necessarily* transgendered is itself problematic. Writers like Jacob Hale and Jack Halberstam have suggested that there may be some overlap in queer communities between transsexual men and butches, an indeterminacy they have termed the 'FTM/butch' borderlands.[24] Referring to the posthumous narrativization of Brandon Teena by transsexual and lesbian writers, Hale points out the near-universal tendency to 'refuse to acknowledge that this person was a border zone dweller: someone whose embodied self existed in a netherworld constituted by the margins of multiple overlapping identity categories'.[25] There is no explicit suggestion in *Written on the Body* that the narrator does not identify within a gender binary, or has crossed any boundaries – indeed, it is equally problematic to assume that the narrator does, and has not.

Yet we cannot easily classify the character as any of the aforementioned real-world gender variant identities either. *Obscuring* a sexed body and gender identification does not mean not having one;

however, some critics have argued otherwise. Philosopher Jennifer Hansen suggests that the character is a cipher, 'intentionally faceless, genderless, and nameless'.[26] Hansen suggests that this ambiguity provides a space for identification for the reader, because 'what happens when we cannot make this character into an object with clear boundaries [...] we are invited to occupy the space of the protagonist ourselves'.[27] But I would like to suggest that in not being marked as/by a gender, the narrator does not merely become a cipher in which the reader inserts themselves. While rewriting an unmarked character as oneself is a distinct possibility, the vast majority of people in the world have a declared gender identity, one which is usually insisted upon quite vigorously if questioned – thus creating a rather large difference between themselves and the narrator.

This becomes clearer if we note that, while the narrator's sexed body is obscured, the gender presentation is by contrast overdetermined. The narrator clearly has multiple points of identification – with gays and lesbians: 'we're dancing together like a pair of 50s homosexuals';[28] with heterosexual couples: 'she's a nice girl, he's a nice boy. It's the clichés that cause the trouble';[29] and sympathizing with heterosexual men with underwear fetishes: 'it's a dicey business going into a boardroom with a large white handkerchief on one side of the suit and a slender pair of knickers in the other'.[30] While cross-gender identification is not unheard of for normatively gendered characters, it is comparatively rare to be so prominent – especially given the narrator's bisexual liaisons. To read the character as a cipher as Hansen does, therefore, is to ignore the fairly predictable heteronormative investments many readers have in maintaining their sex as a point of identification from which desire originates (either towards the same or more usually the 'opposite' sex) – investments which preclude the narrator's eclectic identificatory and desiring practices.[31] Rather than becoming a cipher which is collapsed into the self, the undeclared gender of the narrator instead positions them as supremely other.

In contrast to Hansen, I'd like to suggest that the absence of a declared gender therefore signals not to the audience, but to the transcendent, because the narrator is outside culture, outside the compulsory regimes of sex and gender – and yet is still very clearly embodied. Derrida suggests that negative theology is marked by its usage of 'hyperessentiality', a 'being beyond Being' that retains the Godhead.[32] Much like the body of Winterson's narrator, God is the obscured but still existent in apophatic theology. Indeed, it is arguable that this paradox of being-not-being is the kind of phenomenon that Derrida calls a 'certain possible impossibility'.[33]

Sexual ambiguities and the gift

There is an undoubtedly *sexual* ambiguity in Written on the Body marked by undecidability and apophatic speech. The narrator tells of love affairs with both men ('Crazy Frank') and women – meaning they can be described as bisexual, regardless of their sex. Eve Sedgwick once pointed out that 'some people, homo-, hetero-, and bisexual, experience their sexuality as deeply embedded in a matrix of gender meanings. Others of each sexuality do not.'[34] Despite the occasional self-description as a 'Lothario', the gender ambiguous narrator appears largely absent from the matrix of 'opposite' and 'same' sex-gendered meanings through which sexual 'orientations' are produced. Or, at the very least, they appear to resist a fixed grounding of those meanings to their own body. It could be a serious, non-parodic masculinity by a male-bodied bisexual man. It also may be drawing on undeclared butch conventions from dyke communities, a queer form of seduction that takes particular pride in sleeping with married heterosexual women. Or, the narrator's courtly manner could be a parodic miming of heterosexual romance narrative conventions from the authorial position with no real referent in mind.

Similarly, the sexual identity of the narrator's main paramour Louise is ambiguous to say the least. For instance, if one was to settle upon reading the narrator as female, then one could see Louise as bisexual, given her marriage to Elgin. Or, if one reads the narrator as male, then the relationship perhaps can be seen as one of the 'queer crossings' in heterosexuality that Judith Butler mentions.[35] But, given the aforementioned undecidability of the narrator's gender, the novel therefore opens up but never resolves a series of questions about the sexual identity of Louise as much as about the narrator.

Sexual intercourse itself is marked by apophatic, poetic speech, both for the narrator and their paramours. Curiously for a novel that is about sex and sexuality, *Written on the Body* rarely strays into explicit description of body parts, even for those bodies whose genders are declared. The saying is an unsaying. Louise comes to echo the narrator's own reticence about revealing too much, for 'Louise's tastes had no place in the late twentieth century where sex is about revealing not concealing'.[36] The sex in this novel, therefore, is simultaneously corporeal and transcendent in its obscuring of the gender of the protagonist. Indeed, as a mode of not-revelation, sexuality unsays, wipes over the past. Louise says to the narrator: 'I want you to come to me without a past. Those lines you've learned, forget them.'[37] As John Caputo puts it, 'all of us, from [Gilles] Deleuze to evangelical bible-thumpers, want to be born again'.[38]

Indeed, by grounding itself in the sexual relation, Winterson strays oddly close to another near-contemporary writer. In Jean-Luc Marion's *God Without Being*, in which the sign of 'God' is crossed out in a Heideggerian fashion, the author suggests that, rather than be conceptualized as 'being', it is giving that marks out God. Arguing against the Catholic doctrine of trans-substantiation, he says that: 'presence is no longer guaranteed by the excessiveness of the irreducibly other gift [that is, the Eucharist], as far as assuming the corporeally distinct appearance of an irreducible thing. No doubt there remains an irreducible presence of Christ, but it is displaced from the thing [the host itself] to the community.'[39] Marion ties that giving specifically to the sacraments of the Christian Eucharist. Marion's God appears to undergo a kind of *kenosis*, an emptying out of being, in order to give.

Perhaps heretically I wish to associate this post-metaphysical God of Marion's with the narrator of Winterson's novel. The ontological status of the narrator is as equally unresolvable as that of God in the apophatic tradition. As Marion states, 'love gives itself, even if "his own did not receive him" (John 1:11)'.[40] For the narrator, the lover, however, sex is their sacrament, the means to empty out and to give. 'You have given me everything already',[41] they tell Louise, but it is the narrator who has given up Louise to the care of her husband after her cancer diagnosis. Marion's quote from John becomes particularly pertinent if we think through the novel's queer potentiality, for nothing characterizes queer experiences so much as an unreciprocated giving. Here Sedgwick is exemplary, pointing out the 'frigid response[s] given many acts of coming out'.[42]

Nevertheless, I do not wish to say categorically that the narrator *is* God, indeed such a cataphatic statement is antithetical to negative theology's unsaying. Instead, we can find support for the irrelevance of the distinction between God and other in Derrida's work on the gift in *The Gift of Death*. Referencing Kierkegaard's discussion of the gift of death, which takes place in an unmediated relation between the Jewish patriarch Abraham and God in Genesis 22, Derrida argues that 'what can be said about Abraham's relation to God can be said about my relation without relation to every one (one) as every (bit) other'.[43] He concludes that the infinite alterity of God differs little in the end from the infinite alterity of any other other, suggesting that 'everyone else [...] is infinitely other in its absolute singularity, inaccessibility, solitary, transcendent'.[44]

In a similar fashion, Butler has argued for a certain 'opacity' of the self *even to itself*. She argues that:

> [R]easons course through me that I cannot fully recuperate, that remain enigmatic, and that abide with me as my own familiar alterity, my own private, or not so private, opacity. I speak as an 'I', but do not make the mistake of thinking that I know precisely all that I am doing when I speak in that way. I find that my very formation implicates the other in me, that my own foreignness to myself is, paradoxically, the source of my ethical connection with others.[45]

The self is thus ultimately unknowable in some way. Perhaps the narrator's gender – if they have one – is unknowable to themselves, but it is this opacity that grounds them in the ethical relationship embodied in the sexual relationship with Louise.

Conclusion

As a literary body, gender and sexuality in *Written on the Body* remain ultimately undecidable. It's this undecidability that marks the narrator's body out as transgender in the poetic sense that Halberstam suggests, an open possibility rather than a probability.[46] Gender is instead deferred and displaced – a binary notion of gender is displaced by the ambiguous gender of the narrator, and the final settling of a sex signifier on the body is endlessly deferred by the text. Yet, despite the certain opacity of the self that Butler describes, gender as a lived performative practice that draws on embodied materiality is not so easily obscured as in Winterson's novel. One cannot do without pronouns, documents or social assignment as one sex or the other, cannot unsay the sexed body or sexual relation between bodies. In having a narrator whose gender is impossibly 'undeclared', Winterson participates in the tradition of apophatic speech, queering it to the realm of gender and sexuality, opening up a series of unresolvable ontological questions about gender and sexuality. Grounded in the 'givingness' of sexual intercourse, *Written on the Body* transmutes the impossibly possible sexual relation into something simultaneously immanent and transcendent.

6

Art & Lies: Literature in a Neoliberal Age

First published in 1994, *Art & Lies* may well be Winterson's most difficult book, although as she said on her website 'I am never wilfully obscure, but I do ask for some effort.'[1] Drawing together three characters – a failed priest and doctor named Handel, a female painter called Picasso and the legendary poet Sappho – *Art & Lies* is an ambitious experiment with form concerned with the importance of artistic production. Indeed, the novel concludes with an excerpt of sheet music from Richard Strauss's 'Der Rosenkavalier' – a clear straining at the limits of literary experimentation. Here, as in her other novels, art comes together with sexual truth and religious inspiration. *Art & Lies* is inspired by a simple question: 'how shall I live?' It is that question which I shall argue is a profound challenge to the dominant ideologies of the historical epoch in which she has written, that of *neoliberalism*. This challenge, as elsewhere in Winterson, is articulately in a largely religious language that argues for passion and artistic experience as the defining qualities of a good life.

Neoliberalism, as the Marxist economist David Harvey defines it, is 'a theory of political economic practices that proposes that human well-being can best be advanced by liberating individual freedoms and skills within an institutional framework characterized by strong private property rights, free markets, and free trade'.[2] Although it began in the United States, neoliberalism is a form of political economy whose effects have been felt throughout the world. Neoliberalism has involved the wholesale privatization of government services like healthcare and education, widespread deregulation, the destruction of unions and the marketization of previously common public assets like land, water and even the human genome. Education and healthcare have become expensive commodities rather than basic human rights, with student loan debt exploding in the United States in particular. Meanwhile, work has become casualized, with more short-term contracts than ever before.

We can get at the distinctiveness of the neoliberal era through an analysis of the way it organizes lifeworlds – something profoundly important for Winterson in *Art & Lies*. In his *24/7: Late Capitalism and the Ends of Sleep*, Jonathan Crary has discussed the time of neoliberalism, the ways in which every facet of quotidian existence has been captured by capitalism. He says that we live in:

> [A] switched-on universe for which no off-switch exists. Of course, no individual can ever be shopping, gaming, working, blogging, downloading, or texting 24/7. However, since no moment, place, or situation now exists in which one can not shop, consume, or exploit networked resources, there is a relentless incursion of the non-time of 24/7 into every aspect of social or personal life.[3]

In other words, capitalism in its neoliberal, digital form has effectively removed any 'outside' of the experience to consume. Crary talks about a regime of 'non-stop consumption, social isolation, and political powerlessness'[4] and an individualism that sees consumerist acquisition as the only form of authentic experience. His study notes the ways in which even sleep has become an obstacle for capitalist and governmental institutions like the military to overcome so as to further cultivate both production and consumption. Crary notes the ways in which an apparent novelty of products creates lifeworlds, obscuring broader historical patterns of capitalist arrangements.

As Harvey and Crary trace in their own ways, neoliberalism as a discourse, from the Thatcher and Reagan administrations onwards, forms a kind of hegemonic common sense. Discourses of individual self-reliance have been utilized to justify attacks on the welfare state and, in particular, on welfare recipients – people with disabilities, single mothers and the unemployed. Competition and the social fight of all-against-all have become hegemonic common sense.

But what does that have to do with fiction in general and Winterson specifically? It is relatively easy to see how neoliberalism's ethic of brutal structural adjustment to the welfare state and valorization of self-sufficiency is mappable onto contemporary aesthetics – for instance, the dog-eat-dog world of much reality television and its fictional intensification into violence in *The Hunger Games* series, the grim world of politics in HBO fantasy series *Game of Thrones* etc. *The Hunger Games* and *Game of Thrones* in particular echo the social Darwinist post-2008 austerity era. But, at first glance, it may be hard to see how Winterson's corpus, with its emphasis on passion and authentic experience, reflects its neoliberal cultural context. It was the virtue (and curse) of postmodernism as a term that enabled both the isolation of specific aesthetic qualities (Jameson's pastiche and nostalgia mode, Hutcheon's historiographic metafiction) and the signalling of a new stage of capitalist production, in which the old Marxist distinction between economic base and cultural superstructure has merged, and the economic base is revealed to have been cut through with super-structural cultural logics all along. Indeed, this is still the case with neoliberal forms of capitalism; however, there are no necessary aesthetic conclusions to be drawn from the work of Harvey, Crary or other theorists of neoliberalism.

Instead, echoing Jameson's work on the postmodern, I argue that neoliberalism is a kind of force field through which all kinds of artistic and theoretical impulses make their way. For just as postmodern literature and theory formed the backdrop for Winterson's early work, neoliberalism forms the economic backdrop for Winterson's work in total, which she responds to in notable ways. In her corpus, there are a number of critiques of the neoliberal commodification of the commons. This is developed most explicitly in *Art & Lies*, but can even be found in Winterson's children's book *Tanglewreck*, in which the antagonist Regalia Mason is the CEO of a company called Quanta, which 'made its money by only selling things that people had to buy – like air and water and oil'.[5] In a typically Wintersonian twist, Mason's goal is to commodify time itself, for time (and hence youth, beauty and life itself) has become a resource that can be pillaged from the underprivileged and purchased by the rich.

We can see in Winterson's work, right from the beginning, an interest in resisting the influence of neoliberalism. The rich social world of the northern town of *Oranges Are Not the Only Fruit* – written just as Thatcher began to destroy the social fabric of the post-war era – shows Winterson's dissidence from the individualizing tendency of neoliberalism, and it comes not unsurprisingly in the form of a religious community. Harvey argues that 'stripped of the protective cover of lively democratic institutions and threatened with all manner of social dislocations' the 'disposable workforce' of the neoliberal era 'turns to other institutional forms',[6] including crime, non-governmental organizations (NGOs) and religions. In particular, he notes the return of religion in its evangelical Christian forms in the United States and Latin America, tribalism and fundamentalist in Africa and the Middle East, as well as the emergence of Falun Gong in China. Wendy Brown also notes the renewed emergence of religious rhetoric in supposedly secular countries like the United States. She suggests that, with the undermining of the sovereignty of the neoliberal state by global capital, the waning state 'needs God more as its other sources and powers thin and its territorial grip falters'.[7] But, as religions are transnational, Brown argues their confluence with state power in the United States and Israel is ambivalent, 'and religion is as likely to instrumentalize the nation-state as the other way round'.[8]

I have argued elsewhere that the contemporary landscape of religion is marked by twin trends: the resurgence of 'fundamentalist' forms of religion and the individualist adoption of a New Age influenced 'spirituality'.⁹ Winterson fits neither of those precisely. While her religious frame of reference is often Biblical, it is melded with a rich melange of myths largely taken from the Ancient Greeks. And, although her work is individualist in some ways – a legacy of the elitism of her beloved modernism as much as neoliberalism – it is the individualism not of the capitalist but of those seeking refuge from the deterritorializing (to use the Deleuzian term) flows of global capital, the neoliberal commodification of the entire field of human activity. In Winterson, art, stories, religion and love function as truth-procedures (as Badiou would term them, and as we saw in *The Passion* in Chapter 3); all form a kind of resistance to the commodification of human experience produced by neoliberalism.

Art & Lies

Winterson's sixth novel (including the oft-ignored *Boating for Beginners*), *Art & Lies* is a polemic against the malaise of modern life. Written in 1994, four years after the end of the Thatcher government in the United Kingdom, the novel articulates an early dissent from the cultural consensus of neoliberal ideology that emerged throughout the 1990s. In the novel, a failed Catholic priest and cancer doctor Handel, Picasso (a female artist) and the Greek poet Sappho travel abroad by train, reflecting upon art, romance and family. As their naming might suggest, each of the characters is less a realist character than an idea, a 'voice' as Winterson puts it, engaged in a dramatic monologue reflecting on life in the contemporary. Each reflects on art, love, sex and religion and their role in contemporary society.

It is in the 'voice' of Handel that we find some of *Art & Lies*' most pointed critique of the emerging social form of neoliberalism. He makes clear from the outset his dissent from capitalist society and its structuring of everyday life: 'There is nothing a priori about market forces, nothing about the market that isn't a construction and that couldn't be deconstructed. When I question the great god of the market, my friend, who is an atheist, laughs and calls me a dreamer, but his way of life is a nightmare.'[10] Capitalism, and more specifically the neoliberal mode of capitalism, is instrumentalizing, reducing every facet of everyday life to its ability to be consumed. Moreover, it colonizes the emotional life of its subjects, not merely their hopes and dreams, but their ability *to* dream.

Roughly contemporaneously to Winterson, Marxist critic Fredric Jameson in 'The Antinomies of the Postmodern', has talked about the contradiction between the speed of social change of late capitalism and the standardization of consumer goods, built space, language and even feelings.[11] Jameson notes the confluence of the mass production of goods with the mass production of affect. Similarly, Michael Hardt has noted the ways in which neoliberal economies have tended towards immaterial production – knowledge, code and images.[12] These appropriate the commons, including affect and the biological, the latter of which becomes informatized itself as a form of genetic data available to be patented and reproduced. In short, even the apparently private – the realm of emotion – has become commodified in neoliberalism.

In *Art & Lies*, Winterson takes aim at the standardization of feelings in the neoliberal era. For Handel, it is the banality of media culture that he abhors, for media culture has a kind of anaesthetic effect, numbing the sensibilities of people. He states 'reportage is violence. Violence to the spirit. Violence to the emotional sympathy that should quicken in you and me when face to face we meet with pain.'[13] Handel discusses the ways in which the media rely on 'pornographically' detailed visual images:

> Isn't it well known that nothing shocks us? That the photographs of wretchedness that thirty years ago would have made us protest in

the streets, now flicker by our eyes and we hardly see them? More vivid, more graphic, more pornographic even, is the newsman's brief. He must make us feel, but like a body punched and punched again, we take the blows and do not even notice the damage they have done.[14]

Judith Butler, in *Frames of War*, has talked about the way in which photographs are 'framed' by interpretation, delimiting the field of representability itself. For Butler, writing in the shadow of the War on Terror, there is a 'visual dimension of war [that] relates to the question of whose lives are grievable and whose are not'.[15] The 'wretchedness' that Handel discusses is the kind of 'precarious life' that Butler considers to be the precondition for humanity, our vulnerability towards one another. And so what Handel is bemoaning is an emotional inability of the neoliberal subject to acknowledge precarity, vulnerability and, indeed, basic humanity.

We get another perspective on the emotionally deadening effects of neoliberalism in one of the Sappho segments. Therein, Sappho envisions capitalist labour as a kind of living death, describing the great mass of people on the train in London on their way to work as 'the dead'. She says that 'each man and woman goes to their particular scaffold, kneels, and is killed day after day. Each collects their severed head and catches the train home. Some say that they enjoy their work.'[16] As literary critic Susana Onega notes, *Art & Lies*' 'twentieth century characters are living in an Eliotean wasteland populated by hollow men'.[17] Just as Handel notes the deadening influence of the media, Sappho notes the unhearing masses, whose 'ears are full of the sports pages and the index of the *Financial Times*'.[18] Here again Winterson is critiquing the mass entertainment of the media, as well as the capitalist imperatives that foreground work as the only important site of culture. These living dead remain indifferent to the power of language, to 'the word of power [...] Bible and Law. The ennobling word fit to dub a mouth a poet'.[19]

In *Art & Lies*, the media are far from alone in producing anaesthetized, emotionally stunted subjects. Interestingly, as a doctor himself, Handel holds the disenchantment of scientific epistemology equally to blame in its deadening effects. As a cancer doctor removing breasts, he is responsible for the disfigurement of his patients – dramatized especially by his accidental removal of a woman's healthy breast tissue. Handel notes the gallows humour of his colleagues, 'unrelieved by any spirituality', saying that:

> It is so easy to be a brute and yet it has become rather fashionable. Is that the consequence of leaving your body to science? Of assuming that another pill, another drug, another car, another pocket-sized home-movie station, a DNA transfer, or the complete freedom of choice that five hundred TV channels must bring, will make everything all right? Will soothe the nagging pain in the heart that the latest laser scan refuses to diagnose?[20]

For Handel, science is silent as to ultimate ends, unable to give emotional sustenance to suffering. Instead, pills are used to numb their users to the hollow life of neoliberal capitalism. Surrounded by endless novelty, the individual is nevertheless empty of substance.

In a critique analogous to the critique of neoliberalism in *Art & Lies*, the Marxist critic Slavoj Žižek has suggested that contemporary culture is notable for the ways in which it seeks to curb its 'excessive' dimensions:

> [T]he basic function of enlightened consumerist hedonism is [...] to deprive enjoyment of its excessive dimension, of its disturbing surplus, of the fact that it serves nothing. Enjoyment is tolerated, solicited even, but on the condition that it remains healthy, that it does not threaten our physical or biological stability: chocolate yes, but fat free; Coke yes, but diet; mayonnaise yes but without cholesterol; sex yes, but safe sex.[21]

As Žižek tells it, materiality has a transcendent element that 'serves nothing' that is repressed by 'enlightened' consumerism. Neoliberal capitalism has a kind of anaesthetic effect on people, built from its compulsory consumerism.

As well as the media, labour and science, Winterson situates the emotional numbness of neoliberalism in the heterosexual nuclear family. Picasso's family – and priest – are deaf to her pain caused by her abusive brother. The violence concealed in the heteronormative family form is unbearable for Picasso: 'Who were these people whose bodies were rotting with lies? They were her family.'[22] Indeed, Handel, Sappho and Picasso are all marginal figures estranged from the heterosexual nuclear family. Handel is not only a priest but a castrato, while Sappho and Picasso are both queer women (it is revealed at the end of the novel that the two are lovers). The work of queer phenomenologist Sara Ahmed on emotion may be instructive to compare with Winterson's work. For Ahmed, heterosexual is culturally inscribed as a 'good' object from which happiness is supposed to come. She says: 'The family [...] is a happy object, one that binds and is binding [...] The happy family is both a myth of happiness, of where and how happiness takes place, and a powerful legislative device, a way of distributing time, energy and resources.'[23] Ahmed powerfully argues that happiness is a cultural tautology, one is happy because one's desire is satisfied, one's desire is satisfied because one is happy.

In *Art & Lies*, the culturally sanctioned 'happy' objects of heterosexual desire, family and children are side-lined for a reflection instead of the power of art. Picasso calls newlyweds 'newly-deads'[24] and questions the centrality of the heterosexual nuclear family's ability to satisfy desire. She asks, 'what was desire? Certainly not the safe excursions into family life.' Marriage is 'survival and economics',[25] not passion. The 'til death do us part' of heterosexual marriage makes its participants 'dead to feeling, dead to beauty, dead to all but the most obvious pleasures'.[26] Handel, too, rails against 'romance' – to which he opposes love and beauty: 'Everyone can see how useful romance is. Even the newspapers like romance. They should; they have helped to create it, it is their daily dose of world malaise that poison the heart and mind to such a degree that a strong antidote is required to save what humanness is left in us.'[27] Banal 'romance' in *Art & Lies* can be set against the broader role of passion that we saw in *The Passion* and *Written on the Body*, that 'valuable fabulous thing' that authentic love represents. Passion is not easily won for Winterson, but it represents something profound and life-altering.

Feeling genuine and deep

Art & Lies is not simply a jeremiad about the numbing of modern sensibilities in the neoliberal era, but a call to action to recover true emotion via the realms of art, literature and religion. While he bemoans the emotionally bankrupt sensibilities of his capitalist colleagues, Handel himself 'long[s] to feel, but feeling genuine and deep'.[28] He states, 'that young man in the spotted braces thinks me a fool to listen to opera, to go to Mass, to sit quietly with a book that is better than me'.[29] Here literature emerges as a kind of emotional pedagogy, elevating its readers through its superior otherness, through being 'better' than its reader. Religious practice, too, is a kind of uselessness, a foolishness out of step with the utilitarian neoliberal culture that nevertheless points towards a genuine feeling.

But Winterson avoids Victorian sentimentality about the role of fiction, and stumps for the modernist autonomy of the art work. Right from the epigraph of *Art & Lies* – a 1901 quote from literary critic F.H. Bradley about the autonomy of literature – Winterson signals her intentions to be situated within a canon of modernist writing. Her use of modernist stream of consciousness techniques is most apparent in *Art & Lies*, where the three 'voices' are less characters than archetypes, self-consciously echoing Virginia Woolf's experiments in *The Waves*.

In *Art & Lies*, Winterson outlines an emotional repertoire – art, poetry, opera, (queer) sex and religion – that form a *resistance* to the affective numbing of neoliberalism. Instead, she poses a question, 'how shall I live?' The theme of how to live a good life is a theme as old as the ancient Greeks. Michel Foucault has documented the Greek attention to the care of the self in the third volume of *The History of Sexuality*. Foucault quotes Epicurus, who states 'it is never too early nor too late to care for the well-being of the soul'.[30] Winterson is no doubt cognizant of the theme of the care of the self among the Greeks, gesturing to this with a fantastical tale of the library of Alexandria in which boys live in the shelves of the library, fetching books for patrons in journeys that take weeks. The Alexandrian reference is redoubled in the form of the marvellous book that Handel, Picasso and Sappho find on the train, which is suggested to be made from leaves from the Alexandrian library. In this, Winterson gestures to the entire history of Western letters, suggesting that the archives provide important resources for living in the present.

Picasso's escape from her family, as her name suggests, is in painting. 'The more she looked at pictures the more she saw them as extraordinary events, perpetual events, not objects fixed by time. In the rambly old text books there was talk of "The Divine."'[31] Winterson suggests that there is a dimension of otherness to painting that we might call sacred. As she puts it in her collection of essays *Art Objects*, 'Art, all art, not just painting, is a foreign city, and we deceive ourselves when we think it familiar.'[32] True art cannot be easily assimilated to the banal regime of capitalist media.

But it is not merely the consumption of art that saves Picasso but her own artistic production, her experience of colour: 'she painted herself out of the night and into the circle of the sun'.[33] The sensual experience of colour, of beauty, offers an alternative to the deadening aspects of the heterosexual nuclear family on which capitalism historically has been built. Where the family channels emotion in harmful ways, art is an escape from this emotional death for Picasso. It is suggested at the end of the novel that Picasso is Sappho's lover – lesbian desire again a form of resistance to the banality of heteronormativity for Winterson – but, moreover, the pair's shared artistic practice shows the creativity of queerness.

A poetics of feeling

In *Art & Lies*, as in all of Winterson's work, religion, love and aesthetic beauty are linked, expressions of the same passion. Each is an expression of otherness, a hierophany (to use Mircea Eliade's term). Feminist critic Christy Burns argues that Winterson's work explodes numerous binaries:

> A feminist aesthetics will still remark a binary between self/society, masculine/feminine, critique/eros, but it will also begin to engage a dialectic between such divisions. *Art and Lies'* split between critique and *eros* is an orchestrated interweaving of the two necessary elements of feminist vision. If Winterson utilizes anger to bring about social revision, she also cautions against art as pure rant.[34]

Curiously, although typically for Winterson's critics, Burns does not note the ways in which *Art and Lies* explodes the binary between sacred and secular. Winterson's characters in the novel seek the sublime, ecstasy, jouissance as opposed to pleasure. The novel is an exploration of the transcendent in the immanent. Winterson deconstructs binaries – not merely the gender binary – but between body and spirit, mediated by the alterity represented by art.

But while there are obviously secular implications for Winterson's invocation of authentic feeling under neoliberalism, it is clear that there are religious implications, too. In *Art Objects*, a kind of critical companion of criticism to *Art & Lies*, Winterson states that, 'I grew up not knowing that language was for everyday use. I grew up with the Word and the Word was God. Now, many years after a secular Reformation, I still think of language as something holy.'[35] Sappho talks about the ways in which language supplies an excessive, transcendent quality to life. She says, 'the Word terrifies. The seducing word, the insinuating word [...] I cannot eat my words but I do. I eat the substance, bread, and I take it into me, word and substance, substance and word, daily communion, blessed.'[36] Here language is a kind of sacrament, both exceptional and mundane, transcendent and immanent.

We might call this attention to the holiness of language a kind of theopoetics, a concept which has attracted some critical attention in recent years. Caputo talks about a 'poetics [...] with a heart, supplying the heart of a heartless world. Unlike logos, it is a discourse with pathos, with a passion and a desire, with an imaginative sweep and a flare, one that is, however, not sick but healing and salvific.'[37] Winterson is clearly engaging in a theopoetics, aiming through her experimental techniques to push language past the deadening norms of everyday language use under neoliberalism. We can see this most especially in the Sappho sections, in which the famed poet's work collapses the boundary between sex and language. 'Say my name and you say sex', she says.[38] Here, as in other Winterson novels, sexuality (especially queer sexuality) has a kind of holiness to it. Winterson's tender theopoetics sees language taken from the material world, 'the word shaped out of the substance as the sculpture is shaped from the stone'.[39] Winterson seeks to collapse the boundary between the sign and the referent – a theological project which brings together language and object, sacred and profane, sex and word, spirit and material.

Winterson's interest in revitalizing language is part of a broader project of thinking through how one should live in an unfeeling world.

Art & Lies argues powerfully and provocatively for the redemptive power of art in the recovery of authentic feeling, including religious devotion. The lack of spirituality in neoliberalism is explicitly tied to what Winterson calls 'Hobbes' world, after the philosopher Thomas Hobbes, who theorized that society was a constant war of all against war:

> No, in the dreary Hobbes world, where religion is superstition and the only possible actions are actions of self-interest, love is dead [...] What use is it to love God, to dig my hands in the dark red soil of my home, and feel for it a passion which is not possession but recognition? What use is it to believe that beauty is a Good, when metaphysics has sold her in the market-place?[40]

This societal all-against-all ('the only possible actions are actions of self-interest') perspective has been taken up in neoliberalism with the attack on forms of structural support for the vulnerable (mothers, the elderly, the unemployed, people with disabilities etc.). Here, loving God, recognizing the beauty of the environment and recognizing aesthetic beauty are a kind of resistance to the numbing effects of the neoliberal media culture and the norms of the heterosexual family. Handel finds in religious belief a safe place away from 24/7 consumerism, the alienation of commodity fetishism and art sold in the marketplace. *Art & Lies* taps into Winterson's broader thematics about authentic emotion as holy.

Andermahr suggests that the end of the novel shows the healing power of art for Winterson's characters. She says, 'it seems fitting that the novel ends with nine pages of the score for Strauss' Der Rosenkavalier as the protagonists learn to heal their broken psyches, and begin to sing, both literally and metaphorical [...] drawing on the skills they used in life: poetry for Sappho, painting for Picasso and singing for Handel'.[41] We can see this manifesto for the power of art as typically religious, for the passion which transcends neoliberalism is sacred. In the end, art is a vehicle for authentic emotion in *Art & Lies*, and beauty a form of resistance. While it would be too strong to suggest that Winterson is in any way a socialist (let alone a Communist), it is arguable that the themes of *Art & Lies* offer a clear alternative to the ruling ideologies of neoliberal capitalism. And, although again Winterson is far from a doctrinaire Christian of any form, her work creates space for an experience of the sacred from art.

In a 2005 interview, Winterson said that:

> The problem with rampant capitalism and our loss of religious faith is that the outside now has assumed a grotesque dominance. People have forgotten about the inner life all together. They're almost embarrassed by it because there's nothing there protecting it. Even at their worst, true believers – Muslim, Christian, even Evangelicals – recognize that there is something inside which is not bound by shopping or television. And we need that.[42]

There's a clear argument in the novel for the authentic, for the real, which is a long-standing writerly preoccupation of Winterson's. While she will later, in 2000's *The PowerBook*, play with the possibilities of identity formation in the virtual world of the internet, she never abandons the need for real emotion. This is never an easy task for Winterson – she does after all ask for some effort in reading her books – but it is worth the journey. *Art & Lies* is Winterson's most explicit work of ekphrasis (art about art) but, as well as an argument about the value of art, it is in itself an experience for its reader of the transcendence of the everyday of neoliberal capitalism. If capitalism evaporates the need for an inner life, art can resuscitate this dimension for us. The destruction of the boundary between shopping and not, as described by Crary, shows us the increasing difficulty in finding an outside to capitalist commodification, of affect as much as objects. Neoliberalism has commodified previous pockets of resistance to capitalism. The standardization of feelings noted by Jameson has had a deadening effect on the inner life – and this has only grown in the age of social media (what is an emoticon if not a standardized feeling?). Mediatized romance and emotional pornography flatten out our experiences of emotion, of each other and beauty. There is no space for otherness in the Hobbes world of neoliberal capitalism. *Art & Lies* is a powerful argument for the inner life, for passion, for longing to feel something real and meaningful, for the transcendent and, in the end, for the sacred.

7

Gut Symmetries, New Physics and Kabbalah

Gut Symmetries (1997), Winterson's seventh book (if you count *Boating for Beginners*), shows her development as a religious thinker throughout the 1990s. *Gut Symmetries* is one of Winterson's 'eternal triangles', a bisexual love triangle between Jewish poet Stella, her physicist husband Jove and his lover Alice (also a physicist), who has an affair with Stella, too. Stella is thus the most notable non-Christian character in Winterson's corpus, and the novel is Winterson's most sustained look at non-Christian religious practice.[1] In *Gut Symmetries*, we see Winterson playing with familiar themes such as bisexual love triangles and the transcendental nature of art, but weaving in new elements, too – quantum physics and Jewish mysticism. While reviews of the novel in the 1990s were mixed, it is clear now that *Gut Symmetries* marks a major step in Winterson's ongoing project of creating a religiously inflected body of art.

Quantum physics

At first glance this might seem a surprising idea but, with its two physicist characters, *Gut Symmetries* is also Winterson's most sustained engagement with scientific knowledge. But it should not surprise close readers of Winterson that she would pair science and religion in provocative ways. Literary critics Helena Grice and Tim Woods note that in the novel, 'Winterson establishes a complex and elaborate set of parallels and connections between ancient and medieval theories of matters, Newtonian physics, contemporary cosmology, numerology, the Tarot and astrology.[2] As I have argued throughout this book, Winterson works as a writer in a deconstructive fashion to break down binaries, and this is no less the case with *Gut Symmetries*. *Gut Symmetries* disrupts the boundaries between science and religion, with its interest in physics (the 'gut' of the title refers to Grand Unified Theories, as well as the stomach) and faith, both the kabbalistic practice of Stella's father and the Christian faith of Alice's grandmother. She suggests that there may be correspondences between modern scientific knowledge and religious ideas, for as Alice puts it, 'as an armchair atheist I stumble into God as soon as I get up and walk. I do not know what God is, but I use it as a notation of value.'[3] Noting Alice's interest in the medieval alchemist Paracelsus, who famously said 'as above, so below', literary critic Susana Onega suggests that 'the pun in the novel's title between "gut" (the human belly) and "G.U.Ts." (the acronym of grand unified theories of modern physics) points to a similarly holistic impulse between Renaissance and contemporary physics'.[4] Where the so-called New Atheists like Richard Dawkins and Daniel Dennett see scientific knowledge as precluding even the possibility of religious belief, Winterson's writing problematizes the distinction between the two.

This may be seen as a characteristically postmodern position, echoing Jean-Francois Lyotard's assertion that postmodernism marks the decline of meta-narratives, including the Enlightenment narratives of reason and scientific truth. The hegemony of scientific knowledge collapses in the postmodern era into the 'language games' of experts too specialized to be understood by anyone outside their field. We see the postmodern breakdown of knowledge in *Gut Symmetries*, yet it is *union* that many of the characters, especially Alice and Stella, seek. As Stella puts it, 'the clean boxes of history, geography, science, art. What is the separateness of things when the current that flows each to each is live? It is the livingness I want. Not mummification.'[5] The poet

Stella is no less interested in physics than the physicist Alice, who in turn talks about the 'Miracle of the One' of medieval alchemy.[6]

Grice and Woods argue that 'the novel [...] constantly hinges upon the opposition of the material and the metaphysical, the rational and the irrational. This is mirrored in the natural science of theoretical physics as against the supernatural patterns of the Tarot and the Kabbalah. However, this opposition is also put under severe pressure.'[7] In the character of the physicist Jove, for instance, we see a strictly materialist, atheist approach to the physical world. As he says: 'There is nothing mystical about the universe. There are things we cannot explain yet. That is all.'[8] Jove mocks his wife Stella, who is after all a poet, and her mystical take on the relationship between the material and immaterial. But this kind of disenchanted rationalism is ultimately disavowed by the text, which instead makes a strong case for a mystic approach to science.

In *Gut Symmetries*, Winterson attempts to create a poetics of physics, translating scientific knowledge into aesthetic categories (and vice versa):

> The separateness of our lives is a sham. Physics, mathematics, music, painting, my politics, my love for you, my work, the stardust of my body, the spirit that impels it, clocks diurnal, time perpetual, the roll, rough, tender, swamping, liberating, breathing, moving, thinking nature, human nature and the cosmos are partnered together. Symmetry. Beauty. Perhaps it seems surprising that physicists seek beauty but they have no choice. As yet there has not been an exception to the rule that the demonstrable solution to any problem will turn out to be an aesthetic solution.[9]

This attention to the culturally constructed nature of scientific knowledge may be considered characteristically postmodern, with this deconstruction of the religion/science binary also a deconstruction of sacred/profane and mind/body dualisms. As Alice states: 'Those well built trig points, those physical determinants of parents, background, school, family, birth, marriage, death, love, work, are themselves as much in motion as I am. What should be stable, shifts. What I am told is solid, slips. The sensible strong ordinary world of fixity is a folklore.'[10]

So, while Winterson is dubious about traditional Newtonian physics, she sees in quantum physics the ability to convey a complex – and even contradictory – approach to the world in which it is the role of the observer that helps to determine an outcome (as in Schrodinger's infamous cat). As Onega notes, 'Alice extends this idea to the New Physics where she points to the abandonment of the "either-or" perspective of traditional science for the "both-and" formula stemming from Werner Heisenberg's indeterminacy principle.'[11] No doubt Winterson's deployment of quantum physics as a form of deconstruction would horrify many scientists – as the Sokal/Social Text affair demonstrated – but it misses the point to see Winterson's equations between quantum physics, kabbalah and tarot as making a scientific claim about the material world. As always with Winterson, it is the interior world (the 'cities of the interior', as she puts it in *The Passion*[12]) that must be explored as much as the exterior. Here Winterson has added the truth procedure of the scientific knowledges of physics to the other kinds of truth procedures she had explored earlier in works like *Art & Lies* and *The Passion* – passionate love, art, music and religion.

Kabbalah

From *Oranges Are Not the Only Fruit* onwards, it is clear that Winterson is interested in various kinds of Christianity; however, she is also interested in other religious traditions as well. *Gut Symmetries* marks her most sustained engagement with a non-Christian religion, with its two significant Jewish characters – Stella, a poet, and her father Ishmael, who practices magical kabbalistic experiments in their apartment. Although Stella's mother is not Jewish – and thus were she a real person Stella would not be considered Jewish by *halakha*,[13] Jewish religious law, which considers Jewishness to be only passed down from the mother – it is perhaps more interesting to take the position of the Reform movement of Judaism, which considers patrilineal descent to be sufficient grounds for considering a person Jewish. As the novel puts it, 'Stella was Jewish. Not any old Jewish but Jewish of the House of David. She was Queen Jewish, biblical Jewish, Jewish in silver and kohl.'[14] As such, a consideration of Stella and Ishmael must necessarily include some reflection on the Jewish mystic tradition that Ishmael practices and that Stella has largely lost.

Although the classical rabbinical Judaism of the Talmud and mainstream Jewish practice largely foregoes the metaphysical speculation of theology – which takes a backseat to *halakha* (religious law) and *aggadah* (narratives) in the Talmud – there remain a number of significant exponents of Jewish mysticism. The thirteenth-century collection of books *The Zohar* ('splendour' in Hebrew) comprise one of the key works of the kabbalistic Jewish mystic tradition. While more recently kabbalah has been popularized by the likes of pop singer Madonna, for most of its history kabbalah has been an esoteric pursuit practised by only a few rabbis and Jewish communities. It was only in the eighteenth century in the Eastern European Hasidic movement that ecstatic spiritual practice became a common feature of Jewish religious life on any large scale.

While I have discussed Winterson's negative theology in detail in relation to *Written on the Body* (Chapter 5), it is worth revisiting this subject by focusing specifically on kabbalah – Jewish mysticism – a tradition which intersects with Michel de Certeau's Christian mysticism (which I shall address later in the chapter) in attempting to articulate the unsayable, but which has a number of characteristics specific to the Jewish tradition. Most interestingly, the writings of the kabbalists echo some of

Winterson's earlier preoccupations with the holiness of language. For as Gershom Scholem puts it in his classic study of Jewish mysticism *Major Trends in Jewish Mysticism*, 'language in its purest form, that is, Hebrew, according to the Kabbalists, reflects the fundamental spiritual nature of the world; in other words, it has a mystical value. Speech reaches God because it comes from God.'[15] Although Winterson has written in English, kabbalistic tradition offers some tools for understanding the mysticism of *Gut Symmetries*' Jewish characters.

For Stella the poet, just as for the kabbalists, Jewishness is a property of language that carries with it the esoteric. She says:

> I come from a people to whom the invisible world is everyday present [...] I come from a people who hope against hope, whose melancholy is the outer garment of their mirth. In their celebrations and their mournings, the spirit is the same. I used to speak Yiddish and Hebrew fluently but I have not spoken either for thirty years. What else have I lost?[16]

For Stella, her loss of language is tied to her loss of agency in her marriage, with her unfaithful husband Jove. She imagines her marriage as a form of death: 'what is the moment of death? The hook, the line or the sinker? When I fell in love with him? When I trusted him? When he betrayed me? What kind of death is it?'[17] Heterosexual marriage, as it often is in Winterson (especially in *Written on the Body*), is a kind of living death in which the participants lack the liveliness of romance, artistic endeavour, religious passion. Arguably, then, Stella's sense of the sacred, the invisible as Winterson calls it, has become dulled over the years with her loss of the two languages that mark her Jewish heritage – Yiddish, the language of exile and cultural Jewishness, and Hebrew, the *Lashon HaKodesh*, the holy language of Torah and prayer. As Scholem has noted, 'kabbalists [...] are at one in regarding language as something more precious than an inadequate instrument for contact between human beings'.[18] Although she also makes some reference to Christian traditions, Stella begins her intellectual life by exploring the literature and kabbalistic books in her father's bookstore. Stella's loss, therefore, is a double hit, losing culture and religion, profane and spirit, and it is conflated with the deadening effects of heteronormative marriage. Ishmael tells Stella to watch for 'shadows, signs, wonders'[19] in a hermeneutical quest for meaning, a call to continued interpretation.

What does it mean, therefore, for Stella to belong to a people 'who hope against hope?' There is a kind of messianic longing in this phrase, yet it is less embodied in the form of a concrete Messiah (as it would be in Christianity or Lubavitch Hasidism) than it is for the redemption of history for the Jewish people after so many calamities. Zionists, of course, would imagine the redemption of history to come in the nation-state of Israel, but in this passage and those that follow, Stella contemplates her own mortality as well as the destruction of her marriage through Jove's infidelity. So, although she 'come[s] from a people', it is more of an individualized, existential form of reflection that Stella is engaged in, that of the unique subject, the lover, the poet.

But what of God? Here, as is so often the case with Winterson, God may be considered to be hidden, veiled. Jewish tradition has some interest in negative theology; for instance, the medieval philosopher and Talmudist Maimonides (often known as the Rambam) in particular was known for his apophatic theology. As he puts it in his twelfth-century *Guide of the Perplexed*: 'Know that when you make an affirmation ascribing another thing to Him, you become more remote from Him in two respects: one of them is that everything You affirm is a perfection only with reference to us, And the other is that He does not possess a thing other than His essence.'[20] For the Rambam, we cannot describe God's essence in any meaningful sense, instead we can only use negatives to describe what God is *not*.

And yet, the Rambam appears at times to describe God (a hyper-essentiality of the kind described by Derrida). He cites Exodus 33:20, in which God says that 'man shall not see me and live', arguing that mankind cannot perceive God in his essences, only his actions – *'merciful and gracious, longsuffering and abundant in goodness and truth'.*[21] This apparent contradiction can be resolved by the fact that, as Kenneth Seeskin has put it, for Maimonides:

> [W]e can say that God is merciful to the extent that the order of nature (what God created) exhibits merciful characteristics and angry to the extent that it is harsh toward things that do not take proper care of themselves. The point is not that God possesses emotions similar to ours but that the effects of God's actions resemble the effects of ours.[22]

We can, therefore, praise God, but with the caveat that it is only the *effect* of God in the world that we can apprehend.

Furthermore, although the mysticism of the kabbalah and Hasidism is not precisely negative theology, the kabbalistic idea of *tzimtzum* has a certain familial resemblance to negative theology.[23] Primarily taken from the work of sixteenth-century kabbalistic Isaac Luria, in *tzimtzum*, God 'withdraws' himself, contracting his infinite light in order to perform the work of creation. After the *tzimtzum*, God begins the work of creation, pouring his light into vessels, which shatter, unable to contain the awesome power of God. It is the task of kabbalistically inclined Jews, then, to gather up the shards of light and perform the work of *tikkun*, repairing the world – an idea which continues to inspire Jewish social action today. Although many later kabbalists saw *tzimtzum* as a metaphorical rather than literal process,[24] debating whether there can be any part of space in which God is not, the doctrine retains the trace of *via negativa* mysticism, in which the negativity of God's absence precedes the kabbalistic order of creation.

Winterson suggests that kabbalah is another form of the questioning that underlines scientific discovery, a different grand unified theory to be sure, but one no less valuable. As the neo-Hasidic Jewish theologian

Arthur Green has said, for the kabbalists, 'creation *is* revelation'.[25] And, as Scholem has noted, 'all that lives is an expression of God's language'.[26] Winterson puts it another way in *Gut Symmetries*: 'In the Torah, the Hebrew "to know", often used in a sexual context, is not about facts but connections. Knowledge, not as accumulation but as charge and discharge. A release of energy from one site to another.'[27] Winterson is therefore semantically linking religious knowledge of creation with sexual and scientific knowledges, blending together disparate fields to perceive hidden truths with her mystic's eye. The shards of light in the kabbalistic theory of *tzimtzum* become 'energy' in Winterson's telling, apprehended by both religious and scientific knowledge. In Winterson's Grand Unified Theory, every part of the human experience is fuel for the search for truth.

It should be unsurprising that this collapsing of boundaries of knowledge goes further in *Gut Symmetries* than simply the love triangle that dominates the story, with previous generations engaged in religious and scientific searches of their own. Stella's father Ishmael corresponds with physicists: 'he had been close to Werner Heisenberg whose strange notions of the simultaneous absence and presence of matter had stimulated Papa into investigations of his own. In the paradoxes of the Kabbalah he found the paradoxes of new physics.'[28] He engages in experiments in practical kabbalah – that is to say, white magic. There is much in Jewish tradition that warns of the dangers of practical kabbalah; for example, Chaim Vital in *Shaarei Kedushah* warns that the 'secret mystery' of 'Practical Kabbalah' is 'forbidden to use [...] because it is inevitable that one will also attach to the evil that is joined to good'.[29] And it is a commonly held belief among many Jews that only married men over the age of 40 are mature enough to cope with kabbalah's mystic secrets. It is therefore an esoteric path that Winterson imagines for Ishmael, one on which the secret knowledge of the kabbalah – that is to say, a sacred knowledge – is analogous to the discoveries of new physics, which are mined for their mystical as well as scientific implications. This is underlined by Ishmael's miraculous appearance on the boat at the end of the novel, where he saves Stella's life and then disappears into the ether.

Stella – star – is herself born in a miraculous fashion, on a sledge in New York with a diamond lodged in her spine after her mother swallowed it while she was pregnant. After Stella's mother Uta leaves their apartment to wander around New York on the verge of giving birth, she passes out. Stella's father prays for his unconscious wife to be found by Raphael, an eccentric man with a sledge pulled by huskies.

> Mama never believed that, of course not. That Papa with his shawl, his boxes, his stones, his books, his mutterings, his sleepless years, could pierce events and alter them, that was not science. Not common sense. She thanked chance and Raphael, and only once did she look at Papa as though she might, perhaps, believe him. He said, 'I was able to find you because you were radiant. That night the light in you was strong.'[30]

Here Winterson is clearly referring to the *klippot* of kabbalah, the vessels of light shattered early on in the story of Creation. If the light was strong, therefore, in the kabbalistic reading, Uta must have been strong in holiness and closer to Creation.

Indeed, the recurring motif of the star functions as something of a transcendent gesture in *Gut Symmetries*, signalling beyond the everyday to the sacred. Stella is named after a star that her mother had seen that fateful night, which like all the names in *Gut Symmetries* (Jove is named after the Roman king of the gods, Alice/Alluvia after the sediments of a river) is highly significant. This symbolism both recalls the iconography of the kabbalah, as well as a familiar idea of the New Physics, the fact that we are all made of stars – 'the star-dust of my body'[31] as Winterson puts it.

Christian mysticism

Of course, Winterson is not a Jewish author, and we should not see *Gut Symmetries* as a strictly Jewish-inspired text. Winterson's interest in mysticism can be seen in *Gut Symmetries* both in the Jewish tradition of Stella and her kabbalist father Ishmael, and the metaphysical musings of the main narrator of the novel Alice, who discusses her childhood with a religious Irish grandmother. Christianity remains Winterson's most familiar tool for deconstructing the boundary between sacred and profane. Thus we can get at Winterson's mysticism in *Gut Symmetries* by examining Christian mysticism alongside the Jewish mysticism of the kabbalah. Alice signals the importance of mysticism in the text by talking about her 'grandmother reading from the Bible to a child who hardly understood the words but felt strange intimations of grandeur'.[32]

The French cultural theorist Michel de Certeau has made an important contribution to the study of Christian mysticism in *The Mystic Fable*, wherein he suggests that mysticism emerges out of a religious crisis of language brought about by the emergence of mass writing and literacy. Mysticism as a category is a result of a certain cultural secularization, the disenchantment that Weber discussed in the early part of the twentieth century. Certeau argues that mysticism is an attempt to make the Spirit 'speak', and is distinct from a Biblical exegesis of the word. Certeau argues that mystics pose the question 'what *remains* of the spoken word, without which there is no faith?'[33] Just as for the kabbalists and Winterson, language is holy in Christian mysticism. *Gut Symmetries* can be seen as an attempt at making matter 'speak', just as the mystics try to make the Spirit speak.

This concern to save the spoken word extends to the material world of objects, especially bodies. Certeau defines mysticism as being divided between strange phenomena – the objects of a curiosity sometimes devout, sometimes psychological, psychiatric, or ethnographic – and the Absolute the mystics spoke of, which would be situated in the invisible, regarded as an obscure, universal dimension of man, perceived or experienced as a reality [*un réel*] hidden beneath a diversity of institutions, religions, and doctrines. It is in this second aspect that one draws closer to what Romain Rolland called the 'oceanic feeling'.[34]

Certeau argues that mysticism is reliant on the knowledge of a broadly disenchanted understanding of matter and language as *not* enchanted, against which it then articulates its difference. In contrast to the disenchanted secularists, mystics understand the transcendental and the immanent to be always-already entangled. To put it succinctly, matter itself is sacred for the mystics. Certeau argues that 'the mystics created, from all these psychological or physical "phenomena", a means of articulating the "unsayable" [*indirible*]. They spoke of "something" that could really no longer be said in words.'[35] Mystics ground their writings in the body and language, but gesture beyond both at the same time. Derrida points to this in his work on negative theology, which he says demonstrates a 'hyperessentially, a being beyond Being'.[36] In the plenitude of her language in *Gut Symmetries*, which draws together so many discourses, Winterson points to the ultimate unsayability of the sacred – something which can only be gestured to rather than completely described. But it is not God which is the mystery for Winterson, rather it is the eternal mystery of matter itself.

This is underlined in the miraculous birth of Alice, which revises one of the most well known of Christ's miracles – the feeding of the five thousand in Matthew 14:21. Here, in the towboat after Alice's birth, 'every tug and patrol boat on the stretch surrounded us, but far from sinking we were celebrating. My grandmother called it the Miracle of the Sardines and the Gin. She had only fetched enough for herself but there seemed to be plenty for everyone.'[37]

Art

Furthermore, as a number of writers have noted, Winterson makes major reference to the Tarot in *Gut Symmetries*, with each chapter named after a different card. The chapter in which Stella's birth is recounted is titled 'The Star', where Winterson is playing on the role of the Star in Tarot, which as Onega puts it 'is the major arcana that comes after The Tower in the Tarot pack. It symbolises the Star of Hope among the ruins of the Tower, conveying an irrational, intuitive faith that the tower can be rebuilt on a new base.'[38] It is Stella's role in *Gut Symmetries* to represent the irrational and intuitive, the feminine, with Jove as the masculine, while the more androgynous Alice represents a dialectical resolution of irrational and rational, faith and belief, masculine and feminine.

Stella's irrationality is confirmed by her vocation as a poet. As a child, Stella has a squint, a problem with vision, which her father Ishmael interprets means that she will be a poet. Reflecting on the role of light in artists like Picasso, Matisse and Cezanne, which critics had misinterpreted as 'optical confusion', Stella states that perhaps 'art is an eye problem. What you see is not what you think you see.'[39] Onega notes that 'for Stella, as for Jeanette Winterson, the discourse of art is more truth-revealing than traditional science, geography or history precisely because of its capacity to focus reality from different perspectives, including intangible ones'.[40] Here, as in *Art & Lies*, the artist comes to represent a visionary whose role is in part to tarry with the invisible or scarcely visible. Art has a mediating role analogous to religion which allows us the capacity to 'see' the transcendent, to experience it. As Richard Kearney has put it apropos the modernists Woolf, Proust and Joyce: 'mystery is preserved, even celebrated, not as ecclesiastical dogma but as a mystical affirmation of incarnate existence: Word made Flesh in the ordinary universe.'[41] Winterson's writing is clearly mystical, but in an embodied collapsing of the transcendent and the immanent.

We should not be surprised, therefore, that much of the action of the novel takes place on the ocean, from Alice's birth in a lifeboat, to Alice and Juve's meeting on the QE2 to the final action on the boat in which Juve consumes Stella. The ocean, as I have noted in my analysis of *Boating for Beginners* (Chapter 2), has a metaphysical resonance in which its liquid form seems to deconstruct the finalities of masculine theories of matter – and indeed brings a feminine attention to materiality that problematizes easy binaries. Water can be seen as the very 'stuff' of the sacred in ways familiar to both Jewish and Christian traditions. In its resonance with the womb, water gives birth (just as Alice's mother did) to stories, to knowledge, to energy. In *Gut Symmetries*' references to Jewish and Christian mysticism, then, we can see a new attention to embodied matter – from the gut to the GUT. As Alice notes, in an aphorism that could easily double for Winterson herself, 'religion may lose its appeal but portents are popular'.[42] As a young girl, Alice had made a list of 'correspondences, half true and altogether fanciful, of the earth, the sea and the sky'.[43] Belief in a transcendent God is far from assured for any of Winterson's characters, but attention to the endlessly interpretable material world most certainly is.

Conclusion

As I have argued in this chapter, Winterson's work deconstructs common binaries like science/religion, male/female, heterosexual/homosexual – and even, in *Gut Symmetries*, gin/tonic! But the death of the subject announced by post-structuralism at the high point of the theory in the 1970s and 1980s is nowhere to be seen. Instead, Winterson deconstructs in order to focus on the connection between her characters and broader social ideas. This interest in union, as Mary Holland has shown with regard to American literature,[44] provides evidence of an emerging post-postmodernism, one that continues to blur boundaries but in the name of a humanism that underlines the connections between people. The death of the subject announced by anti-humanist post-structuralism in that sense can be seen to be increasingly out of fashion in both literature and theory. Winterson's work arguably is a significant milestone in an emergent new formation of literature.

Further, in *Gut Symmetries*, Winterson situates the sacred primarily in the here and now world. As Ishmael says to Alice in a deeply improbable (but meaningful) conversation on the boat at the end of the novel: 'Do not mistake me. This is not the afterlife. This is no after life. There is life, constantly escaping from the forms it inhabits, leaving behind its shell. Ashes to ashes, dust to dust. History is in your nostrils.'[45] Although there is some interest in the afterlife in Jewish tradition – the 'world to come' (*olam ha-ba* in Hebrew) – most Jewish practice situates the physical immanent world as primary. It is therefore not surprising that Ishmael would underline the importance of the material world in his final speech, even as his practical kabbalah allows him to escape the boundaries of time and space. Although Winterson allows for the miraculous, in the end it is the very stuff of life and matter that most interests her. *Gut Symmetries* is a poetics of matter, in which it is the very ordinariness of the world that is the most miraculous of all.

8

The PowerBook and Virtual Culture

In *The PowerBook*, Winterson investigates a new way of being: inhabiting cyberspace. In this novel, a gender-ambiguous narrator, named alternately Ali and Alix, tells stories online for a living in a way that blurs the boundaries between real and fake, virtual and actual. Winterson plays with gender norms and embodiment, as well as raising provocative questions about the religious. What does it mean to be human in a virtual age, in which relationships have become mediated by screens? What kinds of opportunities might the virtual provide for the religious? Writing in the year 2000, Winterson attempts a poetics of the newly emergent realm of cyberspace in a typically playful and pleasurable way. Drawing on familiar romances like Lancelot and Guinevere, as well as inventing new tales, Ali tells a multiplicity of love stories given a postmodern twist. For, as she puts it, 'if I start this story [...] it may change under my hands'.[1]

We can see in *The PowerBook* Winterson's continued interest in deconstructing the binary between male and female, heterosexual and homosexual, and of particular interest to this study, religious and secular. But where *Gut Symmetries* saw Winterson deconstructing the boundary between science and literature, here she has moved on to collapsing the border between real and fake, online and offline, narrated story and mundane chat. While *The PowerBook* can be seen to echo many of the concerns of earlier novels, it does so in a new medium. Although Elaine Showalter, for instance, called the novel 'literary junk food' in a review in the *Guardian* newspaper,[2] this arguably underestimates the importance of Winterson's continued investigation of new means of storytelling. In the nearly twenty years since Winterson wrote the novel, few serious authors have attempted a poetics of online life, and few have been as successful as *The PowerBook*.

The virtual

Where Winterson's work of the early 1990s can be seen as postmodern through its historiographic metafiction, and while she never lets go of this thread, in *The PowerBook* Winterson also takes up the Baudrillard-inspired version of postmodernism which many critics have used to analyse the new screen technologies of the 1980s and 1990s – television, personal computers and the internet. French philosopher Jean Baudrillard famously saw the postmodern condition as one of 'simulation', in which reality had become virtual, a new hyperreality. As Baudrillard argues: 'The territory no longer precedes the map, nor survives it. Henceforth, it is the map that precedes the territory.'[3] To put it in the structuralist terms popular in the theory in the 1970s and 1980s: the sign has become disconnected from the referent, the real has become indistinguishable from the virtual. Media has saturated our world, mediating our experience of it (as in that popular response to 9/11: it was 'like a movie') from the start.

So much has changed in the eighteen years since Winterson published *The PowerBook* that it seems hard to believe that the blurring between real and virtual was once an innovation. What was once called Web 2.0 (the internet of blogs, Facebook etc.) and is now just called the internet arguably has intensified the reign of postmodern simulation that Baudrillard saw in the 1980s into something new. Literary critic Alan Kirby has called this new epoch 'digimodernism', a new era in which interactivity has become the norm for textual experience. Kirby suggests that:

[T]he drift of information technology is now toward the phenomenological elimination of the sense of the electronic interface, of the text. Increasingly, perhaps, people will feel that the gulf separating their 'real' and their 'textual' lives has disappeared; the thoughts, moods, and impulses of our everyday existence will translate so immediately into the electronic, textual digimodernist realm that we will no longer be conscious of transference. It won't be a question of oscillating between offline and online, but of hovering permanently between those extremes.[4]

Over the course of time, the perpetual online self that Kirby describes has become more and more seamless, with the data capabilities of smart phones allowing a permanently connected performative self, crafting and curating subjectivity through the omni-present social media.

In *The PowerBook*, Winterson has anticipated this blurring between online and offline lives. Ali tells her customer/beloved: 'This is where the story starts. Here, in these long lines of laptop DNA. Here we take your chromosomes, twenty-three pairs, and alter your height, eyes, teeth, sex. This is an invented world. You can be free for just one night.'[5] I have argued throughout this book that Winterson deconstructs binaries and here in *The PowerBook* there are more – as well as the familiar gender and religious play (of which, more later), the binary between real and virtual is deconstructed. As Andermahr puts it, 'the text demonstrates the possibilities presented by the Internet for shucking off old identities and adopting new ones.'[6] Ali can 'change the story. I am the story.'[7] This can be seen as posthuman in the sense described by theorist Katherine Hayles: 'In the posthuman, there are no essential differences or absolute demarcations between bodily existence and computer simulation, cybernetic mechanism and biological organism, robot teleology and human goals.'[8] In the posthuman world of cyberspace, the lines between real and virtual are blurred. Or, as Ali states: 'the more I write, the more I discover that the partition between real and invented is as thin as a wall in a cheap hotel room'.[9]

Whereas Winterson warned of the anaesthetizing effects of popular media in *Art & Lies*, in *The PowerBook* she appears to more strongly embrace the effects of media for their creative opportunities. Andermahr suggests that 'the structure of the text approximates to a series of "windows", each adding a layer to the narrative so that reading it is analogous to surfing the web'.[10] The chapter headings ('OPEN HARD DRIVE', 'NEW DOCUMENT', 'SEARCH' etc.) reinforce this feeling of the page acting as a kind of screen. The author, as Ali quips, has 'gone interactive' – suggesting that there are narrative possibilities being raised by new forms of media. Cyberspace is imagined by Winterson as a 'world inventing itself' in which 'new landmasses form and then submerge' daily.[11] But far from the death of the author famously announced by Roland Barthes, authorial presence remains, exerting a power over the text and indeed over the reader – for *The PowerBook* is at its heart a story of the romance between reader and author, in which the mediating power of narrative (including religiously inflected narrative) seduces, provokes, heals, reveals.

It should be unsurprising, then, that *The PowerBook* would see Winterson raising old concerns in a new medium. Andermahr suggests the novel is another iteration of Winterson's gender play, with Ali/Alix discarding essentialist ideas of gender. Ali says of gender, 'does it matter? This is a virtual world.'[12] Andermahr goes so far as to call the character transsexual, which seems a little too fixed an idea for the fluid movement online and off between identities and genders – although, as with *Written on the Body*, there seems to be no reason to assume that the character is *not* trans too. Here, as so often in her work, gender is fluid and mutable for Winterson, in a constant state of movement. We might follow Jack Halberstam and call this trans*gender* rather than transsexual.[13] In one of Ali's stories, a young woman in the sixteenth century disguises herself as a male sailor, hiding a precious pair of tulips between her legs. Whimsically, Winterson has the tulips act as a phallus, as Ali becomes the lover of a Princess. She says: 'Then a strange thing began to happen. As the Princess kissed and petted my tulip, my own sensation grew exquisite, but as yet no stronger than my astonishment, as I felt my disguise come to life. The tulip began to stand. I looked down. There it was, making a bridge from my body to hers.'[14] This might be, as Ali's beloved/customer states, 'a terrible thing to do to a flower',[15] but it also demonstrates the creative possibilities of narrative and cyberspace alike. In the baroque swirl of a story within a story, Winterson tells and retells love stories in provocative new ways. While gender and sexuality are never far from her mind, these stories also contain important religious ideas.

A virtual religion

The PowerBook raises the topic of religion through its investigation of the virtual. Literary critic Gavin Keulks argues that 'the novel divides between a mediated "net aesthetic" of competing narratives that collapse spatial and subjectivist relations, and an opposed inspirational moralism that is grounded in humanist pieties about desire, authenticity and integrity'.[16] It is here that we can see an emerging post-postmodern sensibility of the kind described by Mary Holland, one that draws on post-structuralism and humanism equally.[17] It would be tempting to see this humanism as embodying the religious spirit of Winterson's work and discard the virtual wrapping of *The PowerBook* as a now-obsolete form of art. But I think we can see in this novel a religious sensibility in *all* of its frames, not simply its naturalistic elements. The telling of the story, Winterson style, is always as significant as its content.

It is that stylistic evocation of cyberspace that is our guide to the religious import of *The PowerBook*. Mark Taylor takes Baudrillard's work and applies it to the field of the sacred. He says that 'it is obvious that we are living in a time of extraordinary transition: something is slipping away and something is beginning'.[18] The consequences of that transition are linked to the rise of new forms of media: 'When everything is always already mediatized, image becomes real and reality becomes imaginary. In this postmodern culture of images and simulacra, all reality is, in effect, virtual reality.'[19] Taylor suggests that the process of virtualization in contemporary culture may approach 'transsubstantiation'.[20] Indeed, 'even in death – especially in death (God's death as well as what is sometimes called "my own") – God continues to haunt from a distance that grows ever more proximate'.[21]

It is this death of God, for Winterson as much as Taylor, that we can see in virtual culture. I have argued throughout this book that Winterson's writing can be seen as post-secular, as having discarded the transcendental guarantor of meaning that is God. As with Villanelle in *The Passion*, who is 'never tempted by God but likes his trappings', *The PowerBook* has little interest in God as a metaphysical being.[22] To put it bluntly, God is more or less dead for Winterson. In one of the tales that Ali tells, set in a 'muck midden', the narrator asks her mother:

> 'Is there a world beyond here?'
> She shook her head and stretched out her arms end to end.
> 'Nothing but waste and scrap. The earth itself is nothing but a collection of belched rocks and burning gases. We live in a cosmic dustbin.'
> 'Is the lid on or off?'
> 'On. Nobody gets beyond the dustbin.'[23]

The immanence of life is affirmed again here by Winterson, underlining the importance of a life lived for its own sake, rather than a Christian hope for life after death. There is no getting 'beyond' life, no afterlife to await. God will not save Winterson's characters.

And yet, despite discarding much of the figure of God, religious language and culture continue to exert an influence on Winterson's writing all across her corpus. Paradoxically, although Winterson affirms life, there is also a kind of transcending of materiality at work in *The PowerBook*. This has obvious religious implications as well as echoing some of the posthuman rhetoric discussed by Hayles. Christian theologians have long talked about kenosis, the emptying out of Christ's self. The idea of kenosis derives from a single verb, *kenoō* ('I empty') which appears in Philippians 2:

> Your attitude should be the same as that of Christ Jesus: Who, being in very nature God, did not consider equality with God something to be grasped, but made himself nothing, taking the very nature of a servant, being made in human likeness. And being found in appearance as a man, he humbled himself and became obedient to death – even death on a cross! (Phil. 5–8 (New International Version))

The key idea of the passage is that Christ 'made himself nothing', although scholars have long argued over what this emptying might mean. German theologian Jurgen Moltmann argues in *God in Creation* that kenosis is a creative act, saying:

> God 'withdraws himself from himself to himself' in order to make creation possible. His creative activity outwards is preceded by this humble divine self-restriction. In this sense God's self-humiliation does not begin merely with creation, inasmuch as God commits himself to this world: it begins beforehand, and is the presupposition that makes creation possible. God's creative love is grounded in his humble, self-humiliating love. This self-restricting love is the beginning of that self-emptying of God that Philippians 2 sees as the divine mystery of the Messiah. Even in order to create heaven and earth, God emptied himself of all his all-plenishing omnipotence, and as Creator took upon himself the form of a servant.[24]

For Moltmann, kenosis makes possible life itself. God's withdrawal echoes the Jewish kabbalistic idea of *tzimtzum*, discussed previously in Chapter 7 on *Gut Symmetries*. In kenosis, God humbles himself, divesting himself of the power traditionally associated with the divine. God's love, here, is enabled by the very act of becoming more human, more fallible.

What I want to argue in raising the idea of kenosis in this context is that virtual culture might offer a kind of kenosis for its users that we can see in *The PowerBook*. If, as Taylor has suggested, the real becomes virtual and the virtual becomes real online, there is a weakening of the metaphysical presence of the reader/user, whose body becomes bound up in narrative. Winterson's writers and readers in the novel have a fluid existence, endlessly mutable yet always questing to transcend the mundane. 'I'm looking for the meaning inside the data', Ali says.[25] 'We are coming into a dark region. A single word might appear. An icon. This icon is a private Madonna, a guide, an understanding.'[26] While Winterson uses the word understanding rather than faith, I think we can see here a small hope for transcending the mundane, for finding meaning beyond the banal. This is, in John McClure's poignant words, a 'partial faith', one that does not depend on the old God of theodicy for its power and its pleasure.[27] The sacred has been weakened by losing its old stories of metaphysical presence and power, and in their place comes forth a small faith, perhaps only a single word or icon.

Winterson therefore acknowledges the power of the symbol, the power of religious iconography, as a continuing feature of contemporary life. In a short episode of the novel set in Capri in Italy, the *flaneuse* Ali watches a group of people – tourists and locals – playing a game of frisbee. Eventually, the frisbee gets stuck on a statue of the Virgin Mary. When it is retrieved, 'everybody salutes the Madonna. Madonna of the Plastic. Madonna of the Mistake. Madonna who sees all and forgives all. Madonna who can take a joke.'[28] Ali calls the statue of the Madonna and San Antonio 'watchers and guardians of the invisible life'.²⁹ Christian iconography in the novel blurs into the iconography of the web – art as religion, religion as art. 'The invisible life' recalls Handel's musings in *Art & Lies* about the importance of an inner life, one nourished by art, music, literature and religion. Yet this is a jocoserious (to borrow a phrase from James Joyce³⁰) affirmation of the Virgin Mary, one with a smirk and a smile at the portentous seriousness of Catholic representations of the Madonna. This Madonna is plastic, a little bit fake, virtual, part of a frame within a frame – yet also retaining the traditional value of consolation, of forgiveness. The old power of theodicy, the Christianity of metaphysics, has been discarded, leaving something new and more humble in its place.

And yet, despite this affirmation of the surface, Winterson is unwilling to discard depth, too. Ali goes 'deeper than disguise',³¹ and the sacred and sexual implications of 'meatspace' are affirmed. After all, 'meatspace still has some advantages for a carbon-based girl'.³² Moreover, the refrain of the novel 'freedom just for a night' suggests a return to the real, that the play of cyberspace is temporally limited and not to be mistaken for permanence. As Ali puts it in a typically Wintersonian rhapsody: 'All human love is a dramatic enactment of the wild, reckless, unquenchable, undrainable love that powers the universe. If death is everywhere and inescapable, then so is love, if we but knew it.'³³ The twin drives theorized by Freud – sex and death, eros and thanatos – become transmuted into a romanticized view of the universe, one in which love exerts a more profound influence than that allowed for by the sober rationalist Freud.³⁴ Id combines with love for Winterson to produce something essential, something primal.

We can see this in the following quote, in which Winterson returns to the story of Noah explored in *Boating for Beginners* to depict the implausibility of love:

> Imagine it.
> The floodwaters subside and the ark comes to rest on top of Mount Ararat. The dove returns with an olive branch in her mouth.

> [...]
> I look back on it, amazed. I can hardly believe it is there – absurd, impossible testimony to something that never happens.
> But it did happen. It happened to us.[35]

Here romantic love is again equated with the passion embodied by religious narrative, of the impossible. God might be absent, but the impossible nevertheless appears. We can see this as deconstructive in the mode described by John Caputo, 'a movement of transcendence [which] means excess, the exceeding of the stable borders of the presently possible'.[36] Love changes what is possible for Winterson's lovers. Importantly, too, the impossible love event requires testimony, requires a faithful narrative to attest to its occurrence.

Winterson repeats the idea of 'buried hidden treasure' in the novel, in the Muck Midden narratives as well as in Ali's soliloquies, equating it with the elusive quality of love. In the Muck Midden tales, Alix (for she is Alix in this story – 'X marks the spot') is told by her mother that 'she'll get older' and will 'be looking in the wrong place'[37] for the buried treasure. There is a kind of innocence or naivety being affirmed here, in favour of the eternal quest for the love object. Love as an impossible ideal is to be searched for, whether it be for the chance meeting of lovers online, or George Mallory climbing Everest.

So, if there is a transcendental signifier in Winterson, it is in the love object, who is idealized, venerated, quested for. The 'great and ruinous lovers'[38] intertextually woven into *The PowerBook* draw the internet chat between Ali and her customer Tulip into a broader tradition of religiously inflected romantic iconography. In one particularly moving section, the romance between Francesca and Paolo found in Dante is retold by Ali. Paolo is described by Francesca as 'honey in my mouth as I kissed him,'[39] with the connection between sweetness and kissing obliquely referencing the Song of Songs. Paolo is eventually murdered by Francesca's husband, and as he dies he says 'there is no love that does not pierce the hands and feet'[40] – a more explicit reference to Christ's wounds on the cross. Love and suffering are paired for Winterson, inevitably and inextricably linked. Finally, as they both die, Francesca states that 'no one can separate us now. Not even God.'[41] Here again Winterson's lovers use religious language to express a passion that transcends the mundane, the rules of everyday life. This passion for the other recalls key post-structuralist theological themes of the *tout autre*, the otherness of the other that in the end deconstructs the boundary between self and other, and other and God. If this is a theological language Winterson is employing, it is a post-secular one that shows the divine without sovereignty, the sacred without metaphysical being.

The fatalism of *The PowerBook* echoes most strongly that of *The Passion*, but while Ali acknowledges that this is well-trodden ground for Winterson – 'I keep telling this story'[42] – the interweaving of Renaissance romance narratives with religious narrative and contemporary technology and concerns reinvents the story again. The passion of Christ on the cross provides a model for love, one predicated on noble sacrifice, giving and generosity. Although Jacques Derrida has rightly noted that 'no one can die for me if "for me" means instead of me, in my place',[43] a Christian economy of sacrifice suggests that death is substitutable, with the death of Christ 'saving' every believer from, if not the phenomenological experience of death, then its eternal permanence. Arguably, Winterson sees sacrificial love in these Christian terms as a kind of substitute. Love presents a kind of eternal glory, with the memory of the 'great and ruinous lovers' still exerting a power over the present.

One of the recurring motifs of *The PowerBook* is the idea of the Promised Land, which appears in a number of sections of the novel. Here Winterson reworks the story of the Exodus of the Israelite people, who wandered forty years in the desert before finding Eretz Yisrael, the holy land. Winterson retells the story in a satirical fashion, imagining Israelites who look at the plenty of the holy land, its infamous flowing of milk and honey, and recoil:

'Those cattle! Think how much they will need to eat!'
[…] 'And the honey! Honey everywhere!'
'Swarms of gigantic bees! Oy oy oy.'[44]

Where the narrative in Numbers underlines the fear of the Israelite spies of the strength of the inhabitants of the land (Num. 13:31), Winterson suggests that even the fabled milk and honey overwhelmed them. In the end, the Israelites walk away, thinking 'maybe we could find another Promised Land',[45] a cowardice Winterson equates with the married lover unwilling to leave their unhappy relationship. The fear of plentiful produce in Winterson's gloss on the story is a fear of the plenitude of love, for true love – there is no other kind for Winterson – demands an unconditional devotion that recalls the passionate relation to Israel in the Jewish tradition.

Yet, although Winterson mocks the cowardly Israelite spies who recommended turning away from the Promised Land, she retains the metaphor for its power in addressing the love relation. We can see *The PowerBook* as an affirmation of the value of bravery in love. Although 'lions live in the wilderness', Ali wonders 'how else am I going to find the Promised Land, if not by way of the lions?'[46] In the end, the narrative draws together lovers for Winterson, with Ali thinking: 'Go home and write the story again. Keep writing it because one day she will read it.'[47] The value of stories persists even in the mediated world of the internet – perhaps even in *The PowerBook* intensifying and offering endless possibilities for the connective power of storytelling.

As Keulks has noted, Winterson's 'poetics of love [in *The PowerBook*] becomes hopelessly textualized and hypermediated.'[48] As in Baudrillard's theory, there is no outside to the virtual any longer. Although Ali states that 'there's no Netscape Navigator to help me find my way around life',[49] it's clear that the fluid online world has a potential for poetics, a freedom to invent which is just as important as the consolations of 'meatspace'. The Promised Land, the novel suggests, may well come from a combination of online and offline, from the collapsed boundaries between real and virtual. After all, a story told leaves none unaffected, neither reader nor writer. As Ali puts it, 'I warned you that the story might change under my hands. I forgot that the storyteller changes too. I was under your hands.'[50] Ali and Tulip fall in love through the power of narrative, through the textual pleasures afforded by an endlessly rewritable cyber text. There's a sense almost of the story telling itself, drawn on by its own logic.

But where does this logic leave the religious? Winterson states, 'I keep telling this story – different people, different places, different times – but always you, always me, always this story, because a story is a tightrope between two worlds.'[51] This 'you' is arguably the other, recalling Derrida's *tout autre*, the other of infinite alterity, difference in itself. Far from an exhaustion of ideas, Winterson's repetition of the relation between self and other, you and me, even in the guise of different people, places and times, suggests that it is the philosophical problem of the other that preoccupies Winterson. In *Oranges Are Not the Only Fruit*, Jeanette says that 'I miss God. I miss the company of someone utterly loyal'[52] – a model for relating to otherness that still remains in *The PowerBook*'s invocation of idealized love.[53] Love stories as a tightrope between two worlds suggest not only the solitariness of every person, but the movement between different orders of being – transcendent and immanent.

Conclusion

As a heterogenous book made up of a multiplicity of 'frames', of windows, *The PowerBook* anticipates the penetration of everyday life by virtual technologies. Indeed, the love narrative between Ali and Tulip concludes with two possible endings, leaving it up to the reader – 'you choose'.⁵⁴ This undecidability echoes some of the obvious overarching concerns of postmodern literature, inspired by deconstructionists like Derrida. In one, Tulip leaves Ali on a train, in the other she stays on the platform. Interestingly, this ending suggests the open-ended nature of online life, of the endless re-editing of video culture, of the replaying of video games. But it also draws our attention to the impossible quality of love narratives for Winterson, which in a certain sense are eternal, keep recurring, stay open, stay alive forever. The love event, as we saw in *The Passion*, cannot be measured, forced, controlled. Instead, we must welcome the unanticipated, the arrival of something other.

This openness to the other suggests a blurring between the boundaries of self and other, other and the divine. The novel concludes with one final reference to religious tradition – this time the medieval practice of creating illuminated manuscripts. 'Your body is my Book of Hours. Open It. Read It. This is the true history of the world.'⁵⁵ Books of hours were illustrated devotional books, containing a unique combination of prayers and psalms, with books created for wealthy readers often containing elaborate illustrations. In using this reference, Winterson is suggesting the beloved's body to be worthy of devotion, a beautiful object to be worshiped, cherished, read daily. But this is no nostalgia for an outside to the text. In the end, the body of the beloved is caught up in textuality, in the virtual, in an endlessly deferred movement of desire that keeps in play the spark of passion – and the divine.

9

Lighthousekeeping and the Religious Vocation

Although Winterson is a writer who persistently returns to the same preoccupations – a 'hedgehog' writer, as Susana Onega terms her[1] – over time her work nevertheless has evolved. Across her corpus, Winterson returns to the figure of Christian clergy in almost all of her work. From the reverend in *Oranges Are Not the Only Fruit* to Patrick in *The Passion* to Handel in *Art & Lies*, clergy come to represent typically Wintersonian concerns about passion, desire and faithfulness (or faithlessness in the case of the reverend in *Oranges*). *Lighthousekeeping* provides a particularly interesting example, intertwining the religious life with references to Greek mythology, Darwinian evolution and Wagner's opera *Tristan and Isolde*. Indeed, Onega notes that the intertexts in *Lighthousekeeping* are numerous, widening Winterson's range to include classic Victorian narratives like *The Strange Case of Dr Jekyll and Mr Hyde*, Charles Darwin and *Treasure Island*. Further, she notes that 'the title suggests an intertextual relation with Virginia Woolf's *To the Lighthouse*'[2] as well as the epigraphs from Muriel Spark's *Memento Mori* ('remember you must die') and Ali Smith's *Hotel World* ('remember you must live').[3] But, although Winterson has continued to draw on a wide range of sources, some critics at least have noted a change in the tenor of Winterson's writing. Gavin Keulks, for instance, notes that in some ways *Lighthousekeeping* can be distinguished from Winterson's earlier novels, which were more classically postmodernist in their interest in collapsing and confusing boundaries. He says: '*Lighthousekeeping* strives to restabilize linear history, topographical realism, and character motivation. Although Winterson never exempts these forces from postmodern harassment, their effects do distinguish *Lighthousekeeping* from her preceding books.'[4] Winterson's formal experimentation is not as pronounced in this novel and, interestingly, neither are her interests in gender and sexual iconography.

Lighthousekeeping is the story of Silver, an orphan in the modern day, who lives with Pew, a lighthousekeeper who tells her stories about the lighthouse's past. Here, as elsewhere in Winterson's corpus, the power of stories to create life is pre-eminent. Pew tells Silver stories about a reverend called Babel Dark, who had lived in the area almost two hundred years ago, contemporaneously with Charles Darwin (who makes a cameo appearance in the novel). Dark lives a double life as a bigamist, living part of the year in Bristol with his beloved wife Molly and child, and the rest of the year in Salts (the town near the lighthouse) where he serves as the town preacher. Dark's life in Salts is a miserable one, where he violently beats his legal wife, whom he despises. Although he is a far from laudable character, Winterson paints Dark as embodying some of the tensions of the nineteenth-century setting of this story within a story.

As Dark's name suggests, among the many intertexts in *Lighthousekeeping* is the Hebrew Bible story of the tower of Babel. In this story, humanity aspires to the position of God, building a tower stretching up to heaven. As punishment for this impudence, God creates many languages. As Genesis 11 tells it:

> And the LORD said: 'Behold, they are one people, and they have all one language; and this is what they begin to do; and now nothing will be withholden from them, which they purpose to do. Come, let us go down, and there confound their language, that they may not understand one another's speech.' So the LORD scattered them abroad from thence upon the face of all the earth; and they left off to build the city. Therefore was the name of it called Babel; because

the LORD did there confound the language of all the earth; and from thence did the LORD scatter them abroad upon the face of all the earth. (Gen. 11:6–9)[5]

In other words, the story of the tower of Babel is one in which language becomes a barrier between people. We can note the geography of the story: God decides to 'go down', he descends, he enters – creates – a world in which language divides groups of people. He enters the world of immanence. By contrast, to aspire to one language, a holy language, is to aspire to Godliness, which is associated with height, transcendence. There is therefore a movement between the lower and the upper, between heaven and earth, that is coded in linguistic terms.

In naming the character Babel, Winterson is clearly drawing on the Bible story for its power in constructing a narrative of language. Babel struggles to establish a rapport with his parishioners and his wife in Salts, and struggles to communicate beyond himself. He keeps two journals, 'the first, a mild and scholarly account of a clergyman's life in Scotland. The second, a wild and torn folder of scattered pages disordered, unnumbered, punctured where his nib had bitten the paper.'[6] Language divides in nineteenth-century Salts, just as Dark's self is divided. It is only in Bristol, where he is known as Lux – escaping being named *as* Babel – that he is able to connect with others (and that is only temporary, in the end).

We can see this interest in the power of language in Silver's narrative arc, too. Silver's relationship with Pew is a narrative one, with Pew's storytelling showing Silver the power of the word. Winterson has talked glowingly of the oral narratives of the north of England she was raised in, and it is here that we see this culture at work in her writing, through the recurring motif of 'tell me a story' that opens chapters as epigraphs. Pew, and then later Silver, tell stories that appear to construct the world in a typically postmodern fashion. We can see this, for example, in the following exchange between Pew and Silver:

> Tell me a story, Pew.
> What kind of story, child?
> A story with a happy ending.
> There's no such thing in all the world.
> As a happy ending?
> As an ending.[7]

Here and elsewhere Winterson points to the constructed nature of narrative and its ability to frame life into coherent stories.

We can see this interest in constructing narratives through another of Winterson's intertextual references. After leaving Salts, Silver spends her days at a public library,[8] eventually becoming so obsessed with Thomas Mann's novella *Death in Venice* that she follows a librarian home so she can borrow it next. The librarian fears an intruder and calls the police, who arrest Silver and refer her to a psychiatrist when they find out she was stalking the woman for a book. Such a comic episode represents the power of the narrative for Winterson, who shows the obsessive nature of readers. In her more serious moments, however, Winterson sees books as keys for accessing new worlds, for escaping the confines of restrictive communities.

Keulks notes the contradictions between language as connecting medium and language as separating in his work on *Lighthousekeeping*. He states that 'in one paragraph Winterson opposes the "endless babble of narrative" with a desire to "fit the template called language", conjoining obvious biblical analogues with linguistic debates that lie at the heart of structuralism and post-structuralism.'[9] Language both connects and divides in *Lighthousekeeping*, showing Winterson once again as a post-structuralist-influenced writer who reaches beyond the nihilism of postmodernism to create narratives that unite, with a profoundly humanist ethos. Winterson is interested in the power of words to create meaning, to make relationships. And, moreover, it is the Bible which provides a linguistic guide for the reader – the great code, as Northrop Frye has put it.[10] While the story of Babel shows the way that language disconnects, the very familiarity of the stories of the Bible referenced creates a common language, a shared culture between reader and the erudite Winterson. Storytelling here, as elsewhere in Winterson, is a lifesaver.

Light

Lighthousekeeping can be seen as an interplay between the defining metaphors of light and dark, between the light of the lighthouse that gives the book its name and the darkness of Babel Dark, one of the book's most notable characters. Winterson links the idea of light with storytelling, an intertwined vocation. Pew says to Silver:

> 'I can teach you – yes, anybody – what the instruments are for, and the light will flash once every four seconds as it always does, but I must teach you how to keep the light. Do you know what that means?'
> I didn't.
> 'The stories. That's what you must learn. The ones I know and the ones I don't know.'
> 'How can I learn the ones you don't know?'
> 'Tell them yourself.'[11]

The light promised by stories – as Silver puts it: 'Every light had a story – no, every light *was* a story'[12] – must be fostered, kept alive from generation to generation.

Of course, the Christian intertexts of the metaphor of light deployed by Winterson are easily found. In John 8:12, Jesus says that 'I am the light of the world. Whoever follows me will never walk in darkness, but will have the light of life' (New International Version). I do not mean to suggest that Winterson sees the light in *Lighthousekeeping* as an indication of the necessity to believe in Jesus. But, raised by Pentecostals, she is surely attuned to the metaphorical implications of light. Instead, by conflating light with story, Winterson seems to suggest that following the ways of stories – which do include the stories of Christianity, if not exclusively – is a way of lighting up a life. Just as the lighthouse lights a path for ships at sea, so do stories show the way. Silver puts it: 'There it is; the light across the water. Your story. Mine. His. It has to be seen to be believed. And it has to be heard.'[13] These lights, these stories, have a kind of world mapping quality to them – 'these lights connect the whole world',[14] as Pew tells it. Winterson mourns the modern automation of this task, saying 'when the men with computers came to automate it, it would flash every four seconds as it always did, but there would be no one to tend it, and no stories to tell'.[15] The light of storytelling is therefore at risk somewhat with the advent of technology, perhaps bringing us back to the issues raised in *Art & Lies*, where technology has created a banal media culture. The legacy of storytelling is too precious to lose with the advent of technological civilization, Winterson seems to suggest.

But it is not only through a reference to the New Testament that Winterson imagines the metaphor of light in the novel. Onega interestingly suggests that another of the intertexts for *Dark* is the Greek myth of Prometheus – the trickster figure who steals fire from the Gods to give to mankind. She says:

> The comparison of Dark to Prometheus gives an archetypal dimension to his situation, transforming it into a tragic struggle between the archaic forces of wild, naked nature symbolised by Dionysos and expressed in wild emotion or sensation, and the Apollonian forces of reason and ideation, associated with culture, art and subjectivity, that prescribe the mortification and sublimation of those impulses.[16]

This typically complex intertext of Winterson's shows light imagery in a number of different ways. First, Apollo is the Greek god of light and, as Onega notes, is associated with reason and stable order. We can see this light in the 'mild and scholarly' journal of Dark's that he keeps, what we might call the official narrative of his life in Salts.[17] Conversely, the Prometheus reference also suggests the light of fire, a wildness to Dark that, sometimes, illuminates the dark. Dark can be said to steal light from the Gods, giving humanity new knowledge in his discovery of fossils. Winterson's usage of fire, therefore, is multifarious and nuanced.

Darkness

As a man of contrasts, Babel Dark at times is himself covered by a darkness: 'He was like this lighthouse in some ways. He was lonely and aloof. He was arrogant, no doubt of that, and cloaked in himself. He was dark. Babel Dark, the light in him never lit. The instruments were in place, and polished, but the light was not lit.'[18] Babel, especially early in the novel, represents the harshness of established religion – a violent man who beats his wife and offers cold comfort to his impoverished parishioners. Here Winterson shows the ugliness of patriarchal religion, its repression of women, its inability to deliver its promises to its community of believers. There is something dark in Dark, which makes him violent, which makes him far from the Victorian ideal of a clergyman.

So, although Babel was a 'pillar of the community', this is equated by the lighthouse keeper Pew with 'the Bible story of Samson':[19]

> It starts with Samson [...] because Samson was the strongest man in the world and a woman brought him down, then when he was beaten and blinded and shorn like a ram he stood between two pillars and used the last of his strength to bring them crashing down. You could say that Samson was two pillars of the community, because anyone who sets himself up is always brought down, and that's what happened to Dark.[20]

Here Winterson uses the Hebrew Bible intertext of the story of Samson to illuminate the story of Dark. The woman who brought Dark down is his wife Molly, who at the end of the novel finds out Dark's other life, leaving him forever. Moreover, Dark brings down the 'two pillars' of communal life in Salts with his discovery of fossils, which profoundly challenges the Christian norms of the town. Winterson's use of the Samson narrative shows the continued power of Jewish and Christian stories to explain the present.

It is also in his 'wild' journal that we see Dark's darkness, the Dionysiac excesses of passion that Onega rightly points out. This journal symbolizes his impossible urges, his desires for Molly which are associated with a strongly sensual life – so much so that Dark's reason for initially breaking with Molly is because he suspects her lovemaking of being too passionate for a virgin, of having slept with another man. While his legal wife is cultured and 'dull as a day at sea with no wind',[21] Molly is a working-class woman, another of Winterson's redheads, who is passionately in love with Dark. We can see in Dark's journal both light and dark, repression and expression, symbolizing the duelling, opposite qualities of the character.

And yet, for all his darkness, Dark too has something spiritual to offer. We can see in Dark an an-atheist trajectory of the kind described by Richard Kearney.[22] When Dark discovers some fossils that see archaeologists and Charles Darwin coming to Salts to make sense of this discovery, he goes through the despair of atheism: 'God or no God, there seemed to be nothing to hold onto',[23] Dark shows the identity shattering nature of the atheist moment, stating that 'I am splintered by great waves. I am coloured glass from a church window long since shattered. I find pieces of myself everywhere, and I cut myself handling them.'[24] We should note the image of the broken church window, which suggests that not only the self but also organized religion have been torn apart by atheism. Kearney suggests that 'the moment of not-knowing' is one 'available to anyone who experiences instants of deep disorientation, doubt or dread, when we are no longer sure exactly who we are or where we are going.'[25] Here science challenges the easy religious explanations of creation, instead giving us a more difficult narrative about evolution.

Dark and Pew have a conversation about the importance of evolution:

> I woke up in one world and I went to bed in another.
> 'It was but a fancy of his, Reverend. A boy playing with shells.'
> 'No, not a fancy, Pew. The world is older than we can dream it. And how it came about, we hardly know.'[26]

Although this challenges creationist ideas of Biblical literalists who see the world as being only a few thousand years old, the novel suggests that evolution and religious mystery may have some relationship. Sonya Andermahr notes the changeable nature of Winterson's take on evolution, stating that 'Winterson's view of Darwinism emphasizes not so much the fixity of scientific laws but the fluidity, variety and unpredictability of life that they point to.'[27] As the novel tells it, 'Darwin over-turned a stable-state system of creation and completion. His new world was flux, change, trial and error, maverick shifts, chance, fateful experiments, and lottery odds against success.'[28] As in *Gut Symmetries*, the fixed and knowable world of Newtonian physics has been superseded in *Lighthousekeeping*.

Evolution therefore resembles the unfixed, unstable nature of the narrative in Winterson's telling. Although, by her own admission, *Lighthousekeeping* represents a distinct change for Winterson in her relation to postmodern narrativization, there remains a (post-) postmodern interest in the social construction of material life through storytelling. The narrator states that 'in the fossil record of our existence, there is no trace of love. You cannot find it held in the earth's crust, waiting to be discovered.'[29] The intangible nature of love – ever a preoccupation of Winterson's – cannot be found in scientific measurement and it is instead in narrative that we find (and lose) love. Unsurprisingly, this intangibility also will prove to represent something important about the sacred in the novel, too.

Although she is no creationist, Winterson does not leave the story with the social construction of material life. Having deconstructed the binary between science and religion in one way in *Gut Symmetries*, for instance, she disrupts it again in another way in *Lighthousekeeping*. Having moved through a scientific-derived atheism, Dark returns to a more mature, less solid, theism: 'Every wife and sailor had to believe that the unpredictable waves could be calmed by a predictable god. Suppose the unpredictable wave was God?'[30] This return to belief, after unbelief, is a profound one. As W.H. Auden has put it, 'every Christian has to make the transition from the child's "we believe still" to the adult's "I believe *again*". This cannot have been easy to make at any time and in our age it is rarely made, it would seem, without a hiatus of unbelief.'[31] Kearney would see this as an exemplary form of anatheism, a return to God *after* letting go of the God of ontotheology and theodicy, and simple atheistic disbelief, too. 'Genuine faith is never a once and for all; it is something that comes and goes and comes back again.'[32]

We can see this metaphor of God as a wave recalling not only Keller's *creatio ex profundis*,[33] but critical work on the ocean as mystic. Freud famously called mysticism 'the oceanic feeling' in *Civilisation and its Discontents*.[34] Julia Kristeva has argued that this oceanic feeling is an 'intimate union of the ego with the surrounding world, felt as an absolute certainty of satisfaction, security, as well as the loss of our self to what surrounds us and contains us, to a container, and that goes back to the experience of the infant who has not yet established borders between the ego and the maternal body'.[35] This mysticism for Kristeva is a paradoxical experience. On the one hand, it promises security, but on the other this primeval union with the mother shatters the singularity of the unitary self. Belief of this kind is an 'exorbitant more-than-life',[36] excessive and ecstatic. The security promised by the mystical union therefore problematizes easy distinctions between self and other. If we return to *Lighthousekeeping*, then, the 'unpredictable wave' that is God may promise security to those with a more simple form of belief who see God in the calming of waves. But for those who with Auden believe again, the unpredictable wave may be more in the form of the exorbitant more-than-life, may be in the shattering experience of a union which cannot be accounted for, controlled. And it is through language itself that we can communicate this sense of transcendence of the mundane, for as Kearney and Zimmerman have said, 'words, names, metaphors are all that we have to express a deep sense [...] that there is something irreducibly other in our experience'.[37]

Collapsing the binaries

Throughout this book I have argued that Winterson scrambles binaries in her work – between male and female, straight and gay, science and religion, and sacred and profane. In *Lighthousekeeping* we can see this interest in collapsing binary oppositions, too, in the opposition between light and dark. Babel Dark is quite obviously a character whose opposing tendencies lie in tension with one another for most of the novel. In Bristol, he is a loving husband to Molly and father to his child, living in light and going by the name of Lux. There's a Persephone reference to Dark's double life, with his twice-yearly visits to Molly described as 'sixty days a year where life is, where love is, where his private planet tracked into the warmth of the sun'.[38] For the rest of the year, in Salts in Scotland, the main setting of the novel, he lives in darkness, with a wife he beats and parishioners he cannot stand. This runs counter to Victorian morality, which would suggest that Dark's life in Salts is the fine, upstanding one and his life in Bristol the sinful, adulterous one.

It is suggested by the novel that in this bifurcation he is the model for Robert Louis Stevenson's Jekyll and Hyde narrative – one of the nineteenth century's most notorious narratives of the divided self. 'The obvious equation was Dark = Jekyll. Lux = Hyde. The impossible truth was that in his life it was the reverse.'[39] Indeed, Stevenson makes an appearance in *Lighthousekeeping*. Dark says that 'Stevenson had not believed him when Dark told that all the good in his life had lived in Bristol with Molly. Only Lux was kind and human and whole. Dark was a hypocrite, an adulterer and a liar.'[40] When Molly comes to Salts and uncovers Dark's other life, she offers to run away with him to France. Dark refuses, and, unable to live with his decision, walks into the ocean. He says, 'his two months a year with her had made it bearable. She was the air pocket in his upturned boat. Now he had drowned.'[41]

Quite clearly, Dark's inability to reconcile the opposite tendencies in his life leads to his death. Pew asks Silver: '"Do you know the story of Jekyll and Hyde?" "Of course." "Well then – to avoid either extreme, it is necessary to find all the lives in between."'[42] Winterson suggests that the binary between light and dark in the self is one that needs to be reconciled. Dark is no model to imitate. Whereas, in *The Passion*, Henri's dedication to the love event sees him refusing Villanelle's half-hearted love, in *Lighthousekeeping*, Dark's fatal flaw is doubt – his doubting of Molly sets the course for his double life. 'You must never doubt the one you love,'[43] Pew says, commentating on the story of Dark that he is telling Silver. It is Dark whose love for Molly is half-hearted, for right from the start he distrusts her, suspecting her of having other lovers. And yet for all that, she is the woman he loves, if not quite enough to wholeheartedly make a life with only her. He muses to himself: 'why? Why must he live like this? He had got himself caught in a life and the lie had got him caught in a life.'[44]

We can see this thematic of the divided self in the novel as recalling postmodern debates about the construction of identity. The fluidity and in-process nature of the self was a well-travelled critical path in the 1980s and 1990s, whose high points include Judith Butler's theory of the performative gendered self.[45] Yet, although Winterson is clearly indebted to postmodernist – and, going back earlier, to modernist – ideas of the fluid self, the references to nineteenth-century culture point us towards a more realist interest in identity construction at work in this work of Winterson's. Keulks suggests that Silver 'navigates between the polarities of realism and postmodernism embedded within the novel's textual tropes'.[46] So, although their names are intertextual references, the characters of *Lighthousekeeping* are far from the postmodern ciphers of discourse we see in the likes of Thomas Pynchon and Don DeLillo. Winterson's characters are instead fully fleshed ones, whose inner lives are indeed part of the point of the novel.

This attention to character motivation has a deeply religious import, for we can see in the dedication of Pew to his role as lighthousekeeper and storyteller a fidelity to the task of keeping the light alive, in all its permutations. We might describe the task of Pew as a religious vocation, dedicated to maintaining tradition, a repository for stories that creates Salts as a place. Mircea Eliade has talked about the way that sacred space is ontologically solid, against the chaos of a profane nonbeing.[47] While Salts is not a holy space per se in the novel – it is far from being a Temple – it is through the storytelling that Salts appears as a place with a history that connects other stories, from Darwin's theories of evolution to Robert Louis Stevenson's Jekyll and Hyde, to the story of Babel in the Hebrew Bible. We can see these stories through the geographical metaphor deployed by the novel for evolution – as sedimented layers of stories, one on top of another. Space and the self are intimately tied together, for as Pew says, 'there's always been a Pew at Cape Wrath'[48] (the lighthouse at Salts).

This attention to self-making can be seen as creating a 'partial faith', as literary critic John McClure has called it. Although McClure primarily concentrates on the great American postmodernists – Thomas Pynchon, Don DeLillo and Toni Morrison – his argument about the post-secular nature of much contemporary fiction rings true for the English Winterson, even in her ambivalence about postmodernism in *Lighthousekeeping*. McClure says: 'The forms of faith they invent, study and affirm are dramatically partial and open-ended. They do not provide, or even aspire to provide, any full "mapping" of the reenchanted cosmos. They do not promise anything like full redemption.'[49] We can see this partiality at work in *Lighthousekeeping*, with the compromised faith of Babel Dark marking a mature return to faith after the dark night of atheism. We can also see this in the sceptical but loving faith in a story that Pew manifests – a profound interest in making meaning, in connection. And yet, to continue the light metaphor, it is clear from the way in which Winterson glosses the metaphor of the lighthouse that the stories we tell, most notably religious stories, are only a partial illumination. Winterson prefers the metaphor of the flashes of light in the dark, rather than a whole day of sunlight.

Further, there is, as McClure has shown, an open-ended facet to the imagination of religion in much contemporary writing applicable to *Lighthousekeeping* in particular and Winterson's work in general. Dark's invocation of the 'unpredictable wave' of God suggests that there is something that cannot be accounted for. John Caputo would call this an event 'an irruption, an excess, an overflow, a gift beyond economy, which tears open the closed circles of economics'.[50] An event is a moment of grace, something unable to be calculated or earned. Dark clearly does not deserve grace ('Dark was a hypocrite, an adulterer and a liar'[51]), and yet, in a surprisingly orthodox fashion, Winterson gives it to him. His death in the waves brings a kind of peace, if not forgiveness.

It is in this watery finale that we can see this post-secular religion of Winterson, returning to some of the imagery we saw at work in *Boating for Beginners*. Silver describes the Noah narrative as 'part miracle, part madness'[52] – something that she sees, and desires, for herself. For Winterson, there is something very unlikely in the Bible narratives, something passionate and unforeseen. The weakness of God that Caputo speaks of is clearly at work in *Lighthousekeeping*, with Dark's God far from an interventionist God, and with his role as creator of the universe displaced by the scientifically verifiable process of evolution. This is, as we see throughout Winterson's work, a God *after* God, a religion without religion. Creeds and dogma have no place in *Lighthousekeeping*, and they serve Dark poorly. Instead, it is in the individual's own movement through atheism to faith and back again that interests Winterson.

While there is no God of theodicy in *Lighthousekeeping*, no interventionist God, it is the natural world itself that gives meaning in the end. Darwin tells Dark, 'nothing can be forgotten. Nothing can be lost. The universe itself is one vast memory system. Look back and you will find the beginnings of the world.'[53] We can see this as a kind of sacramental imagination, of the sacred in the immanent world of things. The event of God, although it transcends the mundane, takes place in the world of here and now, a post-secular movement that incorporates the scepticism of atheist science and moves beyond it into a kind of aestheticized faith in storytelling. It does not redeem Dark's sins, does not cleanse them, but it does provide the chance for connection still. Storytelling provides the means to draw together past, present and future, a holy vocation that binds people and place. Like the fossils that Dark discovers, the past lives on, but it is only in disconnected fragments, because after all, as Silver says, 'the continuous narrative of existence is a lie'.[54] Winterson's work is, as I've argued, a religion of art, religion in art and art as religion, and this is as true for *Lighthousekeeping* as it is for her earlier works.

10

Climate Change Apocalypse and *The Stone Gods*

In 2007's *The Stone Gods*, Winterson makes her first attempt at a kind of science-fiction writing. In it, she revisits the themes of creation and apocalypse explored earlier in *Boating for Beginners*, but updates them with a more contemporary interest in climate change. The novel is structured in three parts, with the first set in a futuristic planet called Orbus in which climate change has necessitated the discovery of a new planet to live on. The second part is set on Easter Island, and the third in a post-apocalyptic society on earth after a third world war called Post-3 World. The three sections are woven together through a lead character named Billie/Billy Crusoe, whose name suggests one of the key intertextual references in the text. Typical for Winterson's interest in gender play, Billie is a queer woman in the Orbus and Post-3 World segments, and a queer man named Billy in the Easter Island section.

Marxist critic Darko Suvin, writing in the late 1970s, has famously termed science fiction the 'literature of cognitive estrangement',[1] a form that stages the concerns of the culture in which it was written in an estranged way. For Suvin, science fiction is a metaphoric and metonymic literature that extrapolates social and material circumstances into an entire world. We can see in Winterson's embrace of science fiction in *The Stone Gods* an attempt at grappling with contemporary climate change (among other scientific and social trends). This turn towards science fiction is perhaps unsurprising, for as novelist and critic Amitav Ghosh has discussed in his recent *The Great Derangement: Climate Change and the Unthinkable*,[2] serious literary fiction has struggled to depict climate change in a compelling way. There is in Winterson's writing a growing interest in science and technology from the late 1990s with the physics of *Gut Symmetries*, through the virtual world of *The PowerBook* to the full-blown science fiction of *The Stone Gods*.

Critics of *The Stone Gods* have largely concentrated on its invocation of the posthuman and Anthropocene – the interweaving between human and natural that has created an environment dependent on the interventions of capitalism. Timothy Morton has defined the Anthropocene as *'there is no outside-human text'*,[3] showing the profound way in which the environment itself has become cultural. These are worthwhile and relevant themes that I will be supplementing with an analysis of the inevitable religious implications of Winterson's science-fiction narrative. In discussing Winterson's representation of climate change, I will use the lens of apocalypse, as a means of discussing the end of human civilization, and return to the theme of creation in discussing its beginning. I will argue that, in each of the three sections, the novel suggests the movement from creation to apocalypse is a cycle that replays itself in human culture.

Apocalypse

Winterson begins with the end in *The Stone Gods*, with the impending destruction of the planet Orbus from climate change. Billie has a conversation with her boss whose use of corporate jargon shows that, although the novel's concerns are weighty, the prose is written with Winterson's characteristic dry wit:

'Orbus is not dying. Orbus is evolving in a way that is hostile to human life.'
'Ok, so it's the planet's fault. We didn't do anything, did we? Just fucked it to death and kicked it when it wouldn't get up.'[4]

Billie 'can't believe we've reached the end of everything,'[5] that human ingenuity has not found a way out of the climate-change apocalypse. Fredric Jameson has said that it is easier to imagine the end of the world than the end of capitalism, and this is certainly true for many of the characters in *The Stone Gods*. The new planet that Central Power, the country in which Billie lives, has discovered is planned to be right from the start a capitalist society ruled by a board of directors rather than elected officials. One character tells Billie: 'we need infrastructure, buildings, services. If I'm going to live on a different planet, I want to do it properly. I want shops and hospitals.'[6] Winterson suggests that the normative imagination cannot comprehend any society not organized around capitalism and its destruction of the natural world. She notes with great acidity the ways in which capitalism has become increasingly hostile to democracy over the last few decades. And if the earth is becoming hostile to human life, it is only because human life has been hostile to the earth for so long.

It is thus an apocalyptic ending to human civilization through climate change that Winterson imagines. On her website, she wrote, regarding *The Stone Gods*: 'I have said many times that I believe our time to be unique in the history of the world. Either we face our environmental challenge now, or many of us will perish, and much of what we cherish in civilisation will be destroyed. I am sorry to sound apocalyptic, but this is what I believe.'[7]

Although Winterson is far from programmatic in her invocation of environmental issues, there is an apocalyptic tone to the novel that recalls older, Christian-inflected models of imagining the end. Apocalypse has long been the grammar of Western societal destruction, with the book of Revelations in the New Testament a particular key reference point. Although Winterson does not draw on Revelations strongly, there is a key apocalyptic thread running through *The Stone Gods* in its insistent imagining of the end.

Catherine Keller has said that 'we the denizens of Western postmodernity of many possible classes, races, or genders cannot extricate ourselves from apocalypse. We are *in* apocalypse: we are in it as a script that we enact habitually when we find ourselves at an edge, and we are in it as the recipients of the history of social and environmental effects of that script.'[8] Apocalyptic thinking is everywhere, secular and religious, especially and increasingly so in the way we talk about the environment. Apocalypse takes its name from the Greek *apo-kalypso*, meaning an unveiling, a revelation (hence the Biblical book title). As Winterson puts it in *The Passion*: 'What you risk reveals what you value'[9] – as we shall see in the revelations that the end of the world brings in *The Stone Gods*.

Drawing on a reading of Revelation 18 – in which John's apocalypse critiques the 'merchants of the earth' (18:3), Keller notes that apocalypse '"reveals" the global sin as less traditionally religious than economic'.[10] This is equally true for Winterson, too, with the critique of the banality and falsity of neoliberal capitalism Winterson explores in *Art & Lies* intensified and extrapolated in *The Stone Gods*. The novel critiques the 'hi-tech, hi-stress, hi-mess life' of Orbus.[11] Instead, the culture is paedophilic and self-obsessed, mocked relentlessly by Winterson. Here, as in *Art & Lies*, media culture is seen as vacuous and soul-destroying. In one amusing vignette, Winterson satirizes reality television segments by having a contest to win a trip to Planet Blue.

More seriously, contemporary technologies of the self are glossed as narcissistic and empty. Winterson extrapolates current treatments like Botox and plastic surgery into a technology called Fixing, which has given its users eternal youth. Ironically, given the impending 'evolution' of Orbus into a hostile planet, transience and corporeal vulnerability have essentially disappeared from Orbus, with its genetic Fixing and universal plastic surgery. Billie states that 'we all look more or less alike, and there are only two sizes, Model Thin and Model Thinner [...] I look wonderful in a normal sort of way'.[12] Literary critic Luna Dolezal argues convincingly that the novel 'reads in part as a cautionary tale about the effects of biomedicine and consumerism on the body, interrogating the systematic "normative narcissism" that has arisen in late-capitalist postmodern societies in the wake of commercial biotechnologies which work to enhance the body aesthetically'.[13]

Winterson sees this focus on the self leading to a paedophilic society. 'Now that everyone is young and beautiful, a lot of men are chasing girls who are just kids. They want something different when everything has become the same.'[14] So, while sex with a minor aged under 14 is technically illegal in Orbus, it is tolerated – 'sexy sex is now about freaks and children'.[15] Billie talks with a woman who wants to genetically reverse from looking 24 to looking 12 to keep the attraction of her husband, who chases after schoolgirls. There is a kind of moral argument being made here by Winterson in ways that recall the apocalyptic, with a real disgust at the grotesque vampiric society of Orbus. It's hard not to see the destruction of Orbus as justified, with the loss of all moral reasoning. But where Revelations talks of the Whore of Babylon, Winterson puts the blame primarily on normative heterosexuality, which feeds off youth and condemns grown women to invisibility and uselessness.

And so for Winterson the moral corruption of Orbus's paedophilic society is manifested in the climate, the environmental apocalypse a result of a capitalist society bereft of values. The narcissism of Orbus is a direct result of the same advanced capitalism that caused climate change – 'when we destabilized the planet it was in the name of progress and economic growth'.[16] We can see here two interlacing modes of late capitalism: first, the virtualized world of postmodern simulacra as seen in the technologies of the self, and second, the very real destruction of the natural environment in order to produce material for consumption. The natural world is seen as fodder for capitalist appropriation. As Marxist environmental historian Jason Moore has argued, '"*the* economy" and "*the* environment" are not independent of each other. Capitalism is not an economic system; it is not a social system; it is *a way of organizing nature*.'[17] Capitalism for Moore depends on the appropriation of what he calls 'Cheap Nature', which has 'not only compelled capital to seek out new sources of cheap labor-power, food, energy and raw materials, but to enclose the atmosphere as a gigantic ground for greenhouse gases'.[18] While Winterson is no environmental historian, it is clear from *The Stone Gods* that she sees the destruction of the environment as a problem caused by capitalist social organization. Arguably, the Orbus section shows the climate change apocalypse as a man-made problem, and deserved.

The second portion of the novel, set on Easter Island in the time of Captain Cook, perhaps surprisingly replays the same motifs of creation and destruction as the first section. Spikkers, a biracial character with a Dutch father and Easter Island mother, tells Billy Crusoe that the island has been made desolate in order to create the stone gods of the novel's title, the infamous Easter Island statues. '"Is it to be believed", I said, "that an island abundant in all things necessary has been levelled to this wasteland through the making of a Stone God and then by his destruction?"'[19] Mircea Eliade has talked about the way that, for religious people, 'life is not possible without an opening toward the transcendent',[20] suggesting that it is through magical means like the creation of idols (or Stone Gods) that existential chaos is calmed and the world is sacralized. Winterson in some ways accepts the necessity of religious worship, with Billy stating that 'there must be some part of Man that is more than his daily round. Some part of him that will use his profit on a matter of no profit, for the Bible says to us, "What should it profit a Man that he gain the whole World and lose his own Soul?"'[21] Religious worship in this sense appears to be outside the capitalist economy.

And yet, in the Easter Island episode, clearly the production of idols to worship has its cost. Billy suggests that this is a self-destructive impulse that implicates the sacred in the self-destructive cycle of creation and apocalypse. 'I am now satisfied in my mind that the Idols had been worked for magical purposes and in veneration of unseen powers. Rival wars had begun the deadly destruction of vying Idols – for if I can keep my ancestor, while losing you yours, I increase my Mana.'[22] Here Winterson is very aware of the flaws in religions which lead to war, the desire to not only flourish but to destroy the other. The apparent an-economic impulse fuelling the ancestor worship on Easter Island is found to have an economy of its own, one predicated on a cycle of birth and destruction, creation and apocalypse. In placing this narrative sandwiched between two science-fiction episodes about the destruction of the world from climate change and nuclear war, Winterson suggests that the impulse to venerate an idol regardless of cost is little different to the veneration of the self we see in the Orbus section.

Keller suggests that 'apocalypticism straddles the distinction between scribe and prophet',[23] with the apocalyptic narrative demanding to be written. There is something of the prophet in Billie/Billy, as with so many of Winterson's characters. Billie is a dissenter from her/his society in all three sections, an 'eccentric'[24] who refuses prevailing cultural norms. This is most notable in the Orbus section, in which Billie runs a farm, 'the last of its line',[25] a biodome of organic life in a world in which nature has disappeared. She writes with a pencil, reads books, allows herself to grow old – all scandalous behaviour in her society. Billie/Billy faces the apocalypse in full knowledge of the flaws of the societies in which she/he lives, hoping against hope for a better outcome this time.

(Re)Creation

In the first section, after leaving Orbus, Billie goes on a journey to a newly discovered planet called Planet Blue, whose only flaw is that it is inhabited by dinosaurs. Planet Blue is 'green and fertile and abundant, with warm seas and crystal rivers and skies that redden under a young sun and drop deep blue.[26] Such an idyllic, pristine world cannot but help recall the Garden of Eden and the birth of humanity. Indeed, just as there was a fall in the Eden narrative, humanity inevitably 'falls' into its old behaviour. If there is a 'sin' for Winterson in *The Stone Gods*, it's the self-absorption that led to climate change, in all three of the novel's settings. Winterson suggests that the desire for new, unspoiled territory is part of the doomed cycle of creation and destruction of human life, one with deadly results for the environment. In Orbus, 'the last hundred years have been hell. The doomsters and the environmentalists kept telling us we were as good as dead and, hey presto, not only do we find a new planet, but it is perfect for new life. This time, we'll be more careful. This time we will learn from our mistakes.'[27]

Winterson's narrative of the (re)birth of human civilization is not, as Christian theologians would put it, a *creatio ex nihilo*, a creation from nothing. Instead, it is a *creatio ex profundis*, a creation from something, for Planet Blue exists, it does not need to be created by humans (and there is little sense of God as a creator here). Although she does mention a 'world formed out of Nothing,'[28] there is little of the heroic metaphysical creation story of much Christian theology. Winterson imagines an alternative creation story: 'There will be a story of a world held in a walnut shell, cracked open by love's finger and thumb. There will be a story of a planet small as a ball, and a child threw it, or a dog ran away with it, and dropped it on the floor of the Universe, where it swelled into a world.'[29] This is a world created by chance, a cosmic accident. God is absent from the scene, playing no real part in the drama of creation. Indeed, there is no singular narrative, no sense that there is one truth to the birth of the world. Instead, there is a kind of postmodern plurality more akin to oral storytelling than theological speculation.

While, at first glance, there might be little place for the divine in Winterson's creation story, there remains a kind of givenness to nature on Planet Blue, the allure of the unspoiled. On arrival, 'the beauty and strangeness of Planet Blue intoxicated everyone [...] it felt like forgiveness. It felt like mercy. We had spoiled and ruined what we had been given, and now it had been given again.'[30] This idea of forgiveness and mercy is a kind of grace, an undeserved reprieve, yet there is no sense of a God behind it. Instead, it is nature itself, creation itself, that forgives by giving purity. There is a plenitude to Planet Blue that overwhelms the senses, that brings consciousness into a relation with something greater than itself. Eventually, even after the failed attempt at creating a colony on Planet Blue, Spike says that 'nature will work with what we have done',[31] and it is suggested in the Post-3 World section that our earth has been founded on the remains of the Planet Blue colonization.

Susana Onega argues that *The Stone Gods* marks a new phase in Winterson's writing, moving from the passionate singularity of the beloved in earlier romances like *The Passion* or *Written on the Body* to a new ecological consciousness. She states that, 'while in the earlier fictions, the quester's journey invariably takes the form of an individual search for true love, in *The Stone Gods* [...] the search is for a remembered world of pristine beauty and harmony ruled by unbounded love'.[32] Although there is indeed a romance between Billie and the female robot Spike – a *Robo sapiens* as the book puts it – the drama extends beyond the love event of the two to a planetary concern for the entire human race. Of course, this planetary concern remains for Winterson mediated by the love between two – on Planet Blue, between the robot Spike and Billie. This passionate romance between the two lovers on a pristine planet recalls Alain Badiou's idea that 'love is always the possibility of being present at the birth of the world'.[33] Billie does not quest for Spike in the way Wintersonian lovers do in most of her earlier work (e.g. Villanelle and the Queen of Hearts in *The Passion*, Lothario in *Written on the Body*), instead it is a search for authentic ways of living as much as loving.

Billie shows this new concern in the following way, imagining the next phase of civilization on Planet Blue:

> There will be men and women, there will be fire. There will be settlements, there will be wars. There will be planting and harvest, music and dancing. Someone will make a painting in a cave, someone will make a statue and call it God. Someone will see you and call your name. Someone will hold you, dying, across his knees.[34]

So, even after the climate change apocalypse, there is hope for a new society, in all its imperfections. Art and religion remain integral parts of the human experience, as important phenomenologically as love and death. God might be man-made (a statue) but faith remains to sustain humanity.

Indeed, the value of religion lies in its ability to give meaning. As Billy puts it, 'the world must have some covering for its nakedness, and so the simplest things come to impart the greatest significance – a piece of bread becomes a body, a sip of wine, my life's blood.'[35] Billy affirms the transcendent in the immanent, the sacred in the material. Religion – in this case Christianity – performs an important function in sacralizing the world. This sacramental imagination, even in the desolation of the religion-fuelled conflict of Easter Island, is a profoundly life-affirming idea of Winterson's.

This life-affirming philosophy suggests a broader interest in the life of the universe. Once it is clear that they are going to die on Planet Blue, Billie and Spike bury their implements for a future civilization to rediscover – an investment in the future that suggests giving is its own value, even unseen and unacknowledged. This investment in life comes paired with an interesting wrestling with the idea of mortality in the novel, with Billie's and Spike's death on Planet Blue a key moment in the text. After Captain Handsome accidentally causes a new ice age in his attempt to rid Planet Blue of its dinosaurs, Billie and Spike choose to stay on the planet. With the air thick with dust, gradually Spike's solar-powered battery begins to wind down, and she dismantles herself until she is only a head. After much philosophical discussion in the novel of the differences between robo sapiens and humans, finally Spike is 'what she said life would be – consciousness'.[36] And as Winterson shows throughout the novel, life implies death, even for robots, with the broader themes of creation and destruction ever present.

We can see a *creatio ex profundis* in another way in the text, in the third section in the post-nuclear earth called Post-3 World. Billie flees with Spike's head to a city made of the wreckage of human civilization called Wreck City. Winterson describes it thus: 'the bomb damage hasn't been cleared in this part of town, and maybe never will be. People live in the shells of houses and offices, and they build their own places out of the ruins.'[37] This is a creation out of already existing matter, a new social realm made from the scraps of a lost civilization.

We can also see a religious ethos in the way the Post-3 World section imagines community. Where Orbus is a hyper-individualist society, and Easter Island wrought by civil war, Wreck City is occupied by criminals, misfits and, perhaps inevitably, some nuns. 'Wreck City had twenty alternative communities ranging from the 1960s Free Love and Cadillacs, to a group of women-only Vegans looking for the next cruelty-free planet.'[38] In Wreck City, a band of outcasts creates new life outside of the ruling ideas of the MORE corporation, which organizes the post-war society in a hugely restrictive way, in a way that makes space for lesbian vegans as much as for Catholic nuns. In its lawlessness, Wreck City recalls not merely socialist and anarchist ideas of social organization but Christian faith communities. Keller has written about feminist apocalyptic communities such as the Shakers, 'female-led utopias [which] resist – from *within* the codes of apocalypse – the tug of apocalyptic masculinity.'[39] Although Wreck City is not a utopia in the traditional sense, it is arguably a form of resistance to the anaesthetizing effects of the Post-3 World society dominated by the MORE corporation. Authentic community in Wreck City is proffered by Winterson as a space for creative self-expression. This is unusual for Winterson, whose novels more often valorize the visionary individual, in love with art of all kinds as well as its beloved other.

Repetition

The Stone Gods is a text about the repetition of human history. It is worth noting, as does Keller, that 'the last book of the Bible [...] darkly mirrors the first'.[40] In other words, creation and apocalypse are bound together from start to end, Alpha to Omega. Dolezal states that 'overall, the work reads as a parable about the seeming inevitability of humankind's self-destructive impulses, exploring doom-laden repeating histories'.[41] Here the Easter Island section works to show us how these doom-laden histories are bound together through religious forms, and that the creation of any idol puts us on the path to the destruction of the world around us. 'Mankind, I hazard, wherever found, Civilized or Savage, cannot keep to any purpose for much length of time, except the purpose of destroying himself', Billy muses.[42]

Moreover, we can see the seeking after pure, unspoilt territory as a kind of colonialism, something underlined by the references to Captain Cook's diaries in the text. And, of course, the very name of the main character – Billie Crusoe – shows the colonial lineage of the text. Billie/Billy is a survivor of a different order, stuck in a foreign place. This is true for all three sections, with Billie stranded on Planet Blue, Easter Island and Wreck City. In all three settings, Crusoe is (metaphorically) shipwrecked from a more technologically advanced society. Spikkers in the Easter Island section is quite obviously a

Friday analogue, a native who cares for Crusoe on a desert island. This recurring motif suggests an ongoing desire to find new land to conquer and develop, until there is an internal limit (as with the post-nuclear environment of Post-3 World or the ruined climate of Orbus).

And yet, Winterson is, as always, ambivalent about any firm binary. 'Life has never been All or Nothing – it's All and Nothing. Forget the binaries', muses Billie.[43] Winterson neither advocates for the endless search for pure territory or the righteous destruction of the sinful (as a more orthodox Christian might have it). This is, as Onega has persuasively said, a 'complex and deeply traumatised multiverse',[44] and as we know from Freud,[45] trauma repeats. Literary critic Nicola Merola has argued that 'by utilizing the formal strategies of repetition and intertextuality and by constructing a looping narrative that offers no closure and no escape, Winterson positions the reader in a melancholy, dysphoric space'.[46] Yet I think this is too pessimistic a view of the novel, which holds out some hope for the future in the form of love, art and creative community-making.

So, although there is a distinct sense of the deserved destruction of the society of Orbus, at least creation and apocalypse are drawn together into a new repetition that both recalls the past and leaves open the future. As Spike puts it, 'everything is imprinted for ever with what it once was'.[47] Keller has talked about what she calls a counter-apocalypse – a feminist apocalypse that reveals without the misogyny of John's Revelations, with all its talk of whores and so on. 'To stand in some particular fragility of place and time, with one's fragments of community and materialities of gender, and to love life: that is perhaps the only real basis of action against the end of the world'.[48] Keller's counter-apocalypse refuses binaries of good and evil, male and female,[49] just as Winterson destabilizes binaries of her own – not just male and female, but human and nonhuman, beginning and end. As the failed colonization of Planet Blue shows, every ending is another beginning for Winterson.

Conclusion

Over the course of her career, Jeanette Winterson has developed as a writer, responding to new cultural desires and anxieties. From the ambivalent social world of northern towns in the 1960s represented in *Oranges Are Not the Only Fruit* to the experimental digital world of *The PowerBook*, each new book by Winterson has allowed her readers an insight into her extraordinarily rich imagination. Yet throughout she has maintained a persistent interest in the Bible as a source of inspiration, and religious practice as a model for the passionate, expressive life she exhorts her readers to embrace. I have argued that Winterson can be understood as a religious – if a/theological – writer in the following ways: first, a deconstruction of binaries that scrambles the line between sacred and profane; second, she understands religion to be art and art to be a form of religion; third, a mystic attention to language; fourth, a sacramental interest in the material; fifth, an imagination of God without sovereignty or theodicy. Each of these key areas shows Winterson to be a highly significant thinker of the post-secular present, as well as one of the most original writers of her generation.

Deconstructing binaries

Numerous literary critics have discussed the ways in which Winterson deconstructs binaries – most especially gender and sexual boundaries. Gender play and sexual ambiguity are two of the most significant aspects of her writing. And yet, it is clear that these are far from being the only binaries she is interested in problematizing. As she has said in an interview: 'we love to have things in polar oppositions, don't we? Black, white. Good, evil. Male, female. And reason, myth. And somewhere there has to be a way of bringing them together again. And it's probably, if you accept both as genuine ways at arriving at truth, but you don't privilege one above the other.'[1] Here Winterson talks about reason and myth as being in binary opposition that structures our society – an opposition which encompasses the fields of science and religion. Religion is undoubtedly a form of myth for Winterson, which does not mean that it is untrue, precisely. Rather it suggests that the kinds of truths that religion arrives at work to impart meaning for the cultures they circulate within.

Deconstructionist-influenced theologians and philosophers of religion in the last thirty years have troubled the boundary between sacred and profane. Mark Taylor wrote about a/theology in the 1980s, attempting to insert a deconstructive hesitation between atheism and theology.[2] Arguably, Winterson's work as a whole has this kind of hesitation, for at different points her characters approach faith in differing ways – there is no consistency between faith and unbelief in her work. Some characters (like Louie in *Oranges*) have faith, others do not. Still others (like Babel Dark in *Lighthousekeeping*) live in the space between belief and unbelief, between faith and atheism. We can see in Dark a return to faith after the dark night of disbelief prompted by the scientific knowledge of evolution – a mature form of faith that recalls Richard Kearney's anatheism, God after God.[3]

Whatever the case for individual characters, what is clear in Winterson's work is that she takes faith, atheism and agnosticism equally seriously. It is rare to find a writer who maintains this balance for any amount of time. While many writers from fundamentalist backgrounds move from dogmatic belief to dogmatic atheism, Winterson's movement from her restrictive Pentecostal background to being a writer of radical gender, sexual and linguistic experimentation did not discard all of the elements of religious culture. She continues to take seriously the comfort and nourishment that religion provides, even after she has long since left the fundamentalist fold and discarded a belief in an interventionist God. This is especially rare for a queer writer, for she has few peers.

Religion as art/art as religion

Kearney, in his important book of post-secular, post-metaphysical thinking *Anatheism*, has argued for the contemporary relevance of revitalizing our thinking on the boundaries between religion and art.[4] Kearney suggests that we need to understand religion in aesthetic terms – religion as art – and aesthetics in religious terms – art as religion. I have argued throughout this book that we can see a similar blurring between these two domains in Winterson's work. The modernist autonomy of the artwork that Winterson so forcefully argues for in *Art Objects*, to varying degrees, is at work in her creative work, too. *Art & Lies* most especially shows a textual world in which art has its own independent existence. But even in that novel, Winterson's most abstract, she is clearly responding to the political, ethical and aesthetic issues of her age – namely neoliberalism and media culture. Handel's, Sappho's and Picasso's rejection of the banality of neoliberal media culture in favour of an ecstatic experience of art points us towards Winterson's interest in creating sublime, even transcendent, art herself. It is my contention that, in her deconstruction of binaries, Winterson largely succeeds in creating an art of religious import. It is in this sense that Winterson has moved beyond her beloved modernism into postmodernism and post-postmodernism, scrambling codes and returning to the sacred *after* the moment of atheism.

Mystic language

We can see Winterson's work as a modern form of mysticism, which shows the mystery of everyday life. Winterson has said:

> I would not want to live a life that did not have mystery in it. I don't need to know everything. I don't need everything explained to me. I do need to have an imaginative connection with the world I live in, which contains elements of wonder, there's elements of the unknown, elements of the fully mysterious that fires me forward. And I look there to arrive at truth about the human condition, about myself.[5]

This interest in mystery is most apparent in *Written on the Body*, where obscuring the gender of the narrator recalls the negative theology of medieval theologians like Nicholas of Cusa and the more recent deconstructionist-influenced interest in otherness and being in itself in the work of theorists like Jacques Derrida and John Caputo.

But Winterson sees mystery in numerous other ways, too. Think of the birth of Stella in *Gut Symmetries*, the way that her kabbalist father peers through the material world to affect the events of his pregnant wife, rescuing her from the snow. While Winterson allows for a sceptical reading that disallows a supernatural interpretation of events, she also opens up the possibility that there is more beyond the realm of science, that mystic experience may well be a valid way of understanding the world. It is no accident that this mysticism occurs in a book in Winterson's corpus most obviously dedicated to scientific knowledge – the Grand Unified Theories of new physics – which in her hands comes to feel like another form of religious discourse. In the end, for Winterson, there is little difference between science and religion – both are inevitably caught up in style, which renders truth as inextricably cultural and poetic.

Sacramental materiality

We can see Winterson's interest in the sacredness of the material in numerous ways throughout her work, in ways that recall both her interest in gender and sexuality as well as the religious. In *Written on the Body*, it is the body of Louise which is described in intimate, loving detail – not merely in terms of sexuality but in the descriptions of her leukaemia. Here Winterson's prose can be seen as an *ecriture feminine* which writes the female body in all its materiality, including sexually. But this materiality does not refuse the transcendent, does not remove the element of the sacred in an atheistic refusal of anything beyond the measurable. Instead, Winterson draws our attention to matter as a sacrament – Louise's body is a fragment of a greater world in which the transcendent is *in* the immanent.

This concern for the material is evident in *Art & Lies*, in which Handel discusses the disenchantment of 'Hobbes world' neoliberal capitalism – where the sacred has been removed from the material for many people.[6] A continued connection to sacramental materiality is important in the novel. In *Gut Symmetries*, on the other hand, the very meaning of matter is described in a more grandiose fashion through various methods, poetic and religious. New physics, kabbalah and medieval alchemy all tell us various truths about the materiality of the world as well as the bodies of lovers. This inevitability includes an element of mystery and chance, in which the miraculous happens (think of both Alice's and Stella's births, as well as the appearance of Ishmael at the end of the novel).

What is clear from the way Winterson approaches the binary between transcendent and immanent is that the beloved is an orienting device, which gives the lover a place in the world. As queer theorist Sara Ahmed has said, 'to be orientated is also to be turned toward certain objects, those that help us find our way'.[7] Time and time again, the beloved sets a path for the Wintersonian lover, in ways that point beyond the everyday and the banal. The material has a little extra, something more in it that eludes categorization and conceptual capture. The material is the precondition for the love event that we see in *The Passion* and *The PowerBook* especially, in which passion exceeds the category borders. It is here that we can see a deconstructive hesitation between the other and the ultimate other, between the lover and God, which ultimately renders the boundary meaningless.

God without theodicy

Of course, it must be noted that Winterson does not advocate belief of any kind, precisely. Like Villanelle, she takes the comfort and the joy and leaves the rest. Winterson has little patience for the restrictive rules of organized religion. In an interview with Bill Moyers, she said that 'human beings have a need to worship. They have a need to make a God for themselves, of one kind, or another. And that is interesting, because it's about us.'[8] We can see throughout Winterson's writing an interest in the ways in which humans make idols, turning the profane into the sacred. Think of Henri's worship of Napoleon in *The Passion*, and the way romantic love transmutes passion into 'something hol'' in that novel. Little wonder that Henri admits he is using 'Bible words again'.[9] Indeed, it is a recurring motif throughout the novels I have examined in this book that romantic love is a fabulous thing to be quested for (and the repeated use of references to the Holy Grail and Tristan and Isolde narratives make this metaphor quite literal). In the terms of Alain Badiou, romantic love is an event, a truth-procedure.[10] But this is an event that challenges the very name of God, which redraws our conceptions of otherness. As Caputo has said, 'by praying to be visited by the event we put the name of God at risk, for the event not only shocks the closure of the world in the name of God, but it also shocks the name of God itself, exposing the fragility of that name'.[11] Winterson's God, if it exists, is a weak God, a God without theodicy, one that may (or may not) appear. Miracles happen in Winterson, but whether there is a higher being behind those miracles is an open, undecidable question.

Facing the future

I have covered Winterson's writing from the mid-1980s in *Oranges* right through until 2007's *The Stone Gods*. Inevitably, given her steady output, there have been some omissions – most notably her short story collection *The World and Other Places* and the novella *Weight*. More recent work in the horror novel *The Daylight Gate* and a rewrite of Shakespeare's *Winter's Tale* in *The Gap of Time* are arguably less significant than her writing before 2007. While these more recent works have their charms, these have been commissioned books and show less of an interest in religion than her earlier work. It remains to be seen how Winterson will respond to new political and religious circumstances in her future publications. Her work between *Oranges* and *The Stone Gods* shows a varied, multi-faceted interest in religion in ways that challenge simple categorizations of sacred and profane, secular and religious. For now, however, it is enough to state that she remains an important and profound writer of the (post-)religious.

Winterson's writing raises broader questions for the practice of literary criticism. In the past decade, American literary critics Amy Hungerford and John McClure have addressed the post-secular nature of American literature over the past half century, using a religious lens to examine writers of the calibre of Toni Morrison, Thomas Pynchon and Don DeLillo.[12] This is important work which needs to be extended significantly. Winterson represents the vanguard of the return of the religious to postmodern and post-postmodern literature generally, creating a nuanced and significant response to the religious climate of the late twentieth and early twenty-first centuries. Writers as varied as Salman Rushdie and Margaret Atwood, too, are writing religiously inflected novels of great importance.

But, while contemporary literary criticism has absorbed many of the insights on identity politics of gender, sexuality, race and migration, it has yet to properly grapple with religion. The interaction between the aesthetic and the sacred is one of the defining experiences of the contemporary world, encompassing topics as diverse as terrorism, reproductive rights, marriage and the well-being industry. This demands a theoretically fluent, sophisticated form of literary criticism, one that draws on the insights of the critical theory of the last few decades. In order to fully understand contemporary literature, we must address the return of the sacred in the post-secular world. Jeanette Winterson helps us to better comprehend what it means to love, to have sex, to pray, to disbelieve, to believe.

Notes

Introduction

1. Mark C. Taylor, *Erring: A Postmodern A/theology* (Chicago and London: University of Chicago Press, 1984), 6.
2. Taylor, *Erring*, 5.
3. Jeanette Winterson, *The Passion* (New York: Grove, 1987), 63.
4. Ibid., 5.
5. Paul Tillich, *Theology of Culture*, ed. Robert Kimball (London, Oxford and New York: Oxford University Press, 1959), 70.
6. Mark C. Taylor, *About Religion: Economies of Faith in Virtual Culture* (Chicago: University of Chicago, 1999), 1.
7. Richard Kearney, *Anatheism: Returning to God After God* (New York: Columbia University Press, 2011).
8. Terry Eagleton, *Culture and the Death of God* (New Haven and London: Yale University Press, 2014), 174.
9. Jeanette Winterson, *Art Objects* (London and Sydney: Vintage, 1996), 153.
10. Taylor, *About Religion*, 26.
11. Jeanette Winterson, *Why Be Happy When You Could Be Normal?* (London: Jonathan Cape, 2011), 68.
12. Winterson, *Art Objects*, 136.
13. Maria Popova, 'Jeanette Winterson on Time, Language, Reading and How Art Creates a Sanctified Space for the Human Spirit', Brain Pickings (2014), https://www.brainpickings.org/2014/07/21/jeanette-winterson-elinor-wachtel-interview.
14. Laura Doan, ed., *The Lesbian Postmodern* (New York: Columbia University Press, 1994), 154.
15. Jeanette Winterson, *Written on the Body* (London: Vintage, 1992), 10.
16. Northrop Frye, *The Great Code: The Bible and Literature* (San Diego: Harcourt, 1982).
17. Kearney, *Anatheism*, 15.

18 Jacques Derrida, *The Gift of Death*, trans. David Wills (Chicago: University of Chicago Press, 1994), 78.
19 Here Derrida is borrowing from the story of the Akedah, the Binding of Isaac in Genesis 22. Derrida's reading draws on Soren Kierkegaard's powerful work on the story *Fear and Trembling*. Soren Kierkegaard, *Fear and Trembling: Dialectical Lyric by Johannes de Silentio*, trans. Alistair Hannay (London: Penguin, 1985).
20 Derrida, *Gift of Death*, 78.
21 Taylor, *Erring*, 6.
22 Ibid., 5.
23 Elaine Showalter, 'Eternal Triangles: Jeanette Winterson's *The PowerBook* is Lost in Space', *Guardian* (2000), https://www.theguardian.com/books/2000/sep/02/fiction.jeanettewinterson1.
24 Winterson, *Passion*, 158.
25 Jennifer Gustar, 'Language and the Limits of Desire', *Jeanette Winterson: A Contemporary Critical Guide*, ed. Sonya Andermahr (London and New York: Continuum, 2007), 55.
26 Jeanette Winterson, *Art & Lies: A Piece for Three Voices and a Bawd* (New York: Alfred A. Knopf, 1995), 51.
27 Ibid., 74.
28 Christy Burns, 'Fantastic Language: Winterson's Recovery of the Postmodern Word', *Contemporary Literature* 37.2 (1996): 278.
29 See Helene Cixous' foundational feminist text in which she lays forth the argument for *ecriture feminine*, 'The Laugh of the Medusa'. Helene Cixous, 'The Laugh of the Medusa', *Signs* 1.4 (Summer 1976): 875–893.
30 Winterson, *Written on the Body*, 73.
31 In her *Succeeding Postmodernism*, literary critic Mary Holland has compellingly discussed American literature after postmodernism as being marked by a new sincerity and humanism. She says, 'literature today remains postmodern in its assumptions about the culture and world from which it arises, and remains poststructural in its assumptions about the arbitrariness and problems of language, and yet still uses this postmodernism and poststructuralism to humanist ends of generating empathy, communal bonds, ethical and political questions, and most basically, communicable meaning'. Although she

does not discuss the English Winterson, it is clear that this applies to her work, too. Holland does in fact cite DeLillo as one of the writers after postmodernism, a view that is in my opinion erroneous, especially when applied to mid-period works like *White Noise*, which is arguably postmodern *tout court*. Mary Holland, *Succeeding Postmodernism: Language and Humanism in Contemporary American Literature* (New York and London: Bloomsbury, 2013), 3, 17.

32 Michel de Certeau, 'Mysticism', trans. Marsanne Bremer, *Diacritics* 22.2 (1992): 15.
33 I take this reference from Richard Kearney's *Anatheism*, 246.
34 Winterson, *Written on the Body*, 120.
35 In *Otherwise Than Being*, Levinas says, 'subjectivity is being a hostage'. Levinas can be seen as one of the chief inspirations of the 'religious turn' of critical theory as well as post-structuralist influenced theology, both of which inform this work. Emmanuel Levinas, *Otherwise Than Being: Or Beyond Essence*, trans. Alphonso Lingis (Pittsburgh: Duquesne University Press, 1998), 127.
36 Winterson, *Passion*, 123.
37 Jeanette Winterson, *Oranges Are Not the Only Fruit* (New York: Atlantic, 1985), 170.
38 This is a point of disagreement between Kearney and Derrida, with Kearney in *The God Who May Be* searching for guarantees that the stranger will be hospitable. For the more fatalistic Derrida, no such guarantee ever can be given. Richard Kearney, *The God Who May Be: A Hermeneutics of Religion* (Bloomington: Indiana University Press, 2001).
39 Terry R. Wright, *The Genesis of Fiction: Modern Novelists as Biblical Interpreters* (London: Ashgate, 2007), 75.

Chapter 1

1 Eve Kosofsky Sedgwick, *Epistemology of the Closet* (Berkeley: University of California Press, 2008), 1.
2 Sonya Andermahr, *Jeanette Winterson* (Hampshire: Palgrave MacMillan, 2009), 4.

3   Marcella Althaus-Reid, *Indecent Theology: Theological Perversions in Sex, Gender and Politics* (London and New York: Routledge, 2000).
4   Marcella Althaus-Reid, *The Queer God* (London and New York: Routledge, 2003), 43.
5   Chris Boesel and Catherine Keller, eds, 'Introduction', *Apophatic Bodies: Negative Theology, Incarnation, and Relationality* (New York: Fordham University Press, 2009), 4.
6   For an interesting example of the holiness of queer and trans bodies, consider a 2010 safe-sex calendar in Spain, which elicited a significant amount of controversy by using transgender women as models of the Virgin. Where recent popes have condemned the transgender community using the terms of a divinely mandated cissexuality ('cis' as in made in God's image, 'trans' as a perversion of the 'natural' order), such creative moves show that LGBT iconography can draw on religious imagery in interesting and significant ways.
7   Jeanette Winterson, *Oranges Are Not the Only Fruit* (New York: Atlantic, 1985), 4.
8   Susana Onega, *Jeanette Winterson* (Manchester: Manchester University Press, 2006), 22.
9   Judith Plaskow, *Standing Again on Sinai: Judaism from a Feminist Perspective* (San Francisco: Harper & Row, 1990), 20.
10 Michel Foucault, *The History of Sexuality. Volume One: The Will to Knowledge*, trans. Robert Hurley (London: Penguin, 1998), 43.
11 Winterson, *Oranges*, 128.
12 Ibid.
13 Cited in Elaine Pagels, *Adam, Eve, and the Serpent* (New York: Vintage, 1989), 102.
14 It is beyond the scope of this book to investigate more fully religious attitudes towards gender and sexuality, however, it is arguable that Christian attitudes to pre-marital heterosexual sex have softened since the 1960s, even in evangelical circles. Given the surveys on marriage equality, I would speculate that attitudes towards homosexuality, too, have warmed in Anglophonic countries since the 1960s, at least among the laity and among some mainstream churches like the Uniting and

Anglican churches, however, this remains incomplete at the very least and does not necessarily reflect the attitudes of church leaders. The Catholic Church, for instance, clearly remains institutionally homophobic in important ways, as are many evangelical Protestants.

15 Michelle Denby, 'Religion and Spirituality', *A Contemporary Critical Guide: Jeanette Winterson*, ed. Sonya Andermahr (London and New York: Continuum, 2007), 100–113.
16 Winterson, *Oranges*, 104.
17 Ibid., 123.
18 Denby, 'Religion and Spirituality', 103.
19 Onega, *Jeanette Winterson*, 24.
20 Winterson, *Oranges*, 105.
21 Abraham Joshua Heschel, *The Prophets* (New York: Harper Perennial, 2001), xxii.
22 Ibid., 10.
23 Ibid., 7.
24 Northrop Frye, *The Great Code: The Bible and Literature* (San Diego: Harcourt, 1982), 29.
25 Winterson, *Oranges*, 4.
26 Ibid., 10.
27 Ibid., 134.
28 Ibid., 133.
29 Judith Butler, *Gender Trouble: Feminism and the Subversion of Identity* (New York and London: Routledge, 2006), 30.
30 Winterson, *Oranges*, 161.
31 Maria Popova, 'Jeanette Winterson on Time, Language, Reading and How Art Creates a Sanctified Space for the Human Spirit', Brain Pickings (2014), https://www.brainpickings.org/2014/07/21/jeanette-winterson-elinor-wachtel-interview.
32 Heschel, *Prophets*, 19.
33 Winterson, *Oranges*, 17.
34 Ibid., 5.
35 Ibid., 133.
36 Ibid., 164.

37 Uri Wernik, 'Will the Real Homosexual in the Bible Please Stand Up?', *Theology & Sexuality* 11.3 (2005): 55.
38 Winterson, *Oranges*, 173.
39 Ibid., 170.
40 Ibid.
41 Sara Ahmed, *The Cultural Politics of Emotion* (New York: Routledge, 2004), 148.
42 Jeanette Winterson, *The Passion* (New York: Grove, 1987), 72.
43 Winterson, *Oranges*, 127.
44 Althaus-Reid, *Indecent Theology*, 67.
45 The softening of attitudes in some Christian circles that I mentioned is clearly not something mirrored in the imaginary of mainstream churches.

Chapter 2

1 As far as I am aware, Terry R. Wright is the only literary critic who has dedicated much time to the novel: in a chapter of *The Genesis of Fiction: Modern Novelists as Biblical Interpreters* (London: Ashgate, 2007) with some analysis of *Boating for Beginners* among readings of *Oranges* and *Lighthousekeeping*.
2 See http://www.jeanettewinterson.com.
3 Jeanette Winterson, *Boating for Beginners* (London: Minerva, 1990), 66.
4 In a 2006 interview with Bill Moyers, Winterson makes this position clear, that she considers religion to be a form of myth – which does not mean that it is not truth, per se, merely not a rational form of knowledge. Bill Moyers, Jeanette Winterson and Will Power, 'Bill Moyers on Faith and Reason', PBS (2006), https://www.pbs.org/moyers/faithandreason/print/faithandreason103_print.html.
5 John D. Caputo, *The Weakness of God* (Indianapolis: Indiana University Press, 2006), 133.
6 Winterson, *Boating*, 15.

7   Ibid., 28.
8   Judith Plaskow, *Standing Again on Sinai: Judaism from a Feminist Perspective* (San Francisco: Harper & Row, 1990), 20.
9   It is important to note that Judaism has a far more accepting view of transgender Jews, with the official positions of both the Reform and Conservative movements explicitly welcoming transgender people into their communities; however, there is some work to do in Orthodoxy.
10 It is beyond the scope of this book to discuss the representation of Marlene in any real detail. Suffice to say that the idea of a transgender woman wanting to re-attach a penis for decoration is not the most transgender-friendly idea, although it does fit with Winterson's broadly comic approach to bodies in the text – Gloria's mother loses an arm in an accident played for laughs.
11 Winterson, *Boating*, 27.
12 Translation from Midrash Rabbah, *Genesis*, vol. 1, trans. H. Freedman (London: Soncino, 1983).
13 Sonia Maria Melchiorre, 'Winterson's Adaptations for the Stage and the Screen', *Jeanette Winterson*, ed. Sonya Andermahr (London and New York: Continuum, 2007), 131.
14 Ibid., 30.
15 Gloria's mother Mrs Munde may be seen as an exception to this, for she seems to sincerely believe in God and draw some strength from him. Even in parodying fundamentalist religion, Winterson always holds out some possibility for authentic spiritual experience.
16 Ibid., 91.
17 Ibid., 14.
18 Wright, *Genesis of Fiction*, 82.
19 Winterson, *Boating*, 71.
20 See Freud's *The Future of an Illusion* for his most extended encounter with religion. Sigmund Freud, *The Future of an Illusion*, trans. J.A. Underwood and Shaun Whiteside (London: Penguin, 2004).
21 Catherine Keller, *Face of the Deep: A Theology of Becoming* (London and New York: Routledge, 2003).

22 Ibid., 9.
23 Saint Augustine, *Confessions* (London: Penguin, 1961), 282.
24 Ibid., 284.
25 We know from Derrida in *Of Grammatology* what kind of dangers the supplement can bring, especially the infamous discussion of Jean-Jacques Rousseau's use of the term 'supplement' in the chapter 'That Dangerous Supplement'. The supplement 'intervenes or insinuates itself *in-the-place-of*; if it fills, it is as if one fills a void'. Jacques Derrida, *Of Grammatology*, trans. Gayatri Chakravorty Spivak (Baltimore: Johns Hopkins University Press, 1976), 141–164 (145).
26 Jacques Derrida, *Writing and Difference*, trans. Alan Bass (New York and London: Routledge, 2001), 86.
27 Keller, *Face*, 10.
28 Caputo, *Weakness*, 62.
29 Keller, *Face*, 15.
30 Luce Irigaray, *Marine Lover of Friedrich Nietzsche*, trans. Gillian C. Gill (New York and London: Columbia University Press, 1991), 12.
31 Ibid., 27.
32 The obvious example being the anthropomorphic 'Mother Earth' occasionally conjured up by environmentalists or New Age religions.
33 Irigaray, *Marine Lover*, 37.
34 Augustine, *Confessions*, 283.
35 Famously advanced in her *Powers of Horror*. Julia Kristeva, *Powers of Horror: An Essay on Abjection*, trans. Leon S. Roudiez (New York: Columbia University Press, 1982). I deal with Kristeva in greater depth in Chapter 4's discussion of *Sexing the Cherry*.
36 Winterson, *Boating*, 91.
37 Ibid., 152.
38 Ibid., 155.
39 Ibid., 158.
40 Ibid., 160.
41 Ibid., 159.
42 Ibid., 160.

Chapter 3

1. Sonya Andermahr, 'Reinventing the Romance', *Jeanette Winterson: A Contemporary Critical Guide*, ed. Sonya Andermahr (London and New York: Continuum, 2007), 97.
2. While there would seem to be little difference semantically between 'passion' and 'romance', Handel in *Art & Lies* rails against romance as manufactured feeling, inauthentic and banal. It is unclear to what degree overall Winterson shares that sentiment, however, there appears to be something of a preference for the language of passion rather than romance in Winterson. Jeanette Winterson, *Art & Lies: A Piece for Three Voices and a Bawd* (New York: Alfred A. Knopf, 1995).
3. Sociologist Anthony Giddens examines the development of discourses of romantic love in the nineteenth century. Giddens thus sees the entirety of the twentieth century as leading to the development of the 'plastic sexuality' of today and the popularization of what he calls the 'pure relationship' – a romantic relationship between equals, freed of the demands of either reproduction or survival. The movement out of the closet by gays, lesbians and bisexuals also developed the pure relationship, extending romantic love to a historically unacknowledged group. For Giddens, then, 'love breaks with sexuality while embracing it'. See Anthony Giddens, *The Transformation of Intimacy: Sexuality, Love and Eroticism in Modern Societies* (Cambridge: Polity, 1992), 2, 48.
4. Sociologists Ulrich Beck and Elisabeth Beck-Gernsheim talk about what they call 'individualization'. Ulrich Beck and Elisabeth Beck-Gernsheim, *Individualization: Institutionalized Individualism and Its Social and Political Consequences* (London: Sage, 2001). For Beck and Beck-Gernsheim, life 'loses its self-evident quality' (8), noting that 'we live in a world in which the social order of the national state, class, ethnicity and the traditional family are in decline' (22). The twin factors of neoliberalism and globalization combine to atomize the modern subject into its most basic form – the individual. Where once people were born into broad groupings like class or religion, today these must

be actively chosen from among the proliferation of 'lifestyle' choices. As Beck and Beck-Gernsheim note, 'whatever we consider – God, nature, truth, science, technology, morality, love, marriage – modern life is turning them all into "precarious freedoms"' (2).

5   Alain Badiou, with Nicholas Truong, *In Praise of Love*, trans. Peter Bush (London: Serpent's Tail, 2012), 28.
6   Alain Badiou, *Ethics: An Essay on the Understanding of Evil*, trans. Peter Hallward (New York: Verso, 2001), 123.
7   Badiou, *In Praise*, 6.
8   Ibid., 7.
9   Badiou, *Ethics*, 122.
10 Badiou, *In Praise*, 41.
11 Ibid., 37.
12 Ibid., 42.
13 Alain Badiou, *Saint Paul: The Foundation of Universalism*, trans. Ray Brassier (Stanford: Stanford University Press, 2003), 54.
14 Ibid., 4.
15 Badiou, *In Praise*, 24.
16 Otto coined this term at the beginning of the twentieth century in *The Idea of the Holy*. Rudolph Otto, *The Idea of the Holy: An Inquiry into the Non-rational Factor in the Idea of the Divine and Its Relation to the Rational* (London: Oxford University Press, 1923).
17 Jeanette Winterson, *The Passion* (New York: Grove, 1987), 55.
18 Ibid., 90.
19 Ibid., 94.
20 Ibid., 64.
21 Ibid., 95.
22 Ibid., 94.
23 Roland Barthes, *A Lover's Discourse: Fragments*, trans. Richard Howard (London: Vintage, 2002), 228.
24 Winterson, *Passion*, 145.
25 Winterson, *The PowerBook* (New York: Vintage, 2000), 220.
26 Ibid., 95.
27 Ibid., 63.
28 Ibid., 72.

29 Ibid., 13.
30 Michelle Denby, 'Religion and Spirituality', *A Contemporary Critical Guide: Jeanette Winterson*, ed. Sonya Andermahr (London and New York: Continuum, 2007), 105.
31 Winterson, *Passion*, 144.
32 John D. Caputo, *The Weakness of God* (Indianapolis: Indiana University Press, 2006), 4.
33 Ibid.
34 Ibid., 2.
35 Gilles Deleuze, *The Logic of Sense*, trans. Mark Lester and Charles Stivale (London and New York: Continuum, 2004), 169.
36 Winterson, *Passion*, 27.
37 Ibid., 13.
38 Ibid., 146.
39 Ibid., 159.
40 Ibid., 145.
41 Badiou, *In Praise*, 61.
42 Caputo, *Weakness*, 5.
43 Winterson, *Passion*, 155.
44 Ibid., 13.
45 Ibid., 10.
46 Zygmunt Bauman, *Liquid Modernity* (Hoboken: Wiley, 2013).
47 Wendy Brown, *Regulating Aversion: Tolerance in the Age of Identity and Empire* (Princeton and Oxford: Princeton University Press, 2006), 45.
48 Jeanette Winterson, *Art Objects* (London and Sydney: Vintage, 1996), 110.
49 Ibid., 111.
50 Ibid., 112.
51 Ibid., 117.
52 Michel Foucault, *The Will to Knowledge: The History of Sexuality*, trans. Robert Hurley (London: Penguin, 1990), 17.
53 Giddens, *Transformation of Intimacy*, 2.
54 Emily McAvan, *The Postmodern Sacred: Popular Culture Spirituality in the Science Fiction, Fantasy and Urban Fantasy Genres* (Jefferson: McFarland, 2012).

55 Mircea Eliade, *The Sacred and the Profane: The Nature of Religion*, trans. Willard Trask (Orlando: Harcourt, 1959), 11.
56 Caputo, *Weakness*, 102.
57 Alain Badiou, *The Century*, trans. Alberto Toscano (Cambridge: Polity, 2007), 64.

Chapter 4

1 Jeffrey Jerome Cohen, ed., 'Monster Culture: Seven Theses', *Monster Theory: Reading Culture* (Minneapolis and London: University of Minnesota Press, 1996).
2 Barbara Creed, *The Monstrous-Feminine: Film, Feminism and Psychoanalysis* (London and New York: Routledge, 1993), 7.
3 Helena Grice and Tim Woods, 'Winterson's Dislocated Discourses', *Jeanette Winterson*, ed. Sonya Andermahr (London: Continuum, 2007), 35.
4 There is little interest in disturbing historical narratives in the same way in Winterson's most recent books *The Daylight Gate* (London: Arrow, 2012) and *The Gap of Time* (London: Hogarth, 2015). While *The Gap of Time* is an interesting rewrite of Shakespeare's *The Winter's Tale* – itself a play with a missing chunk of time in the middle – one could not say that this is precisely a postmodern text. There are few of the stylistic philosophical and narrative pyrotechnics of Winterson's early work in *Gap*, which is a much more straightforward update of Shakespeare's story. That Winterson has little interest in postmodern thematics two decades later is hardly a cause for fault – contemporary fiction in general has moved on from the familiar (maybe even exhausted) postmodern tropes of historiographical metafiction and pastiche – but it is a significant change over time in her writing.
5 Jeanette Winterson, *Sexing the Cherry* (New York: Grove, 1989), 24.
6 Susana Onega, *Jeanette Winterson* (Manchester: Manchester University Press, 2006), 82.
7 Sonya Andermahr, *Jeanette Winterson* (Hampshire: Palgrave MacMillan, 2009), 72.

8   Jane Haslett, 'Winterson's Fabulous Bodies', *Jeanette Winterson: A Contemporary Critical Guide*, ed. Sonya Andermahr (London and New York: Continuum, 2007), 42.
9   Julia Kristeva, *Powers of Horror: An Essay on Abjection*, trans. Leon S. Roudiez (New York: Columbia University Press, 1982), 70.
10 Ibid., 58.
11 Susan Stewart, *On Longing: Narratives of the Miniature, the Gigantic, the Souvenir, the Collection* (Durham and London: Duke University Press, 1993) 70.
12 Sara Martin, 'The Power of Monstrous Women: Fay Weldon's *The Life and Loves of a She-Devil* (1983), Angela Carter's *Nights at the Circus* (1984) and Jeanette Winterson's *Sexing the Cherry* (1989)', *Journal of Gender Studies* 8.2 (1999): 201.
13 Stewart, *On Longing*, 71.
14 Winterson, *Sexing*, 34.
15 Ibid.
16 Onega, *Jeanette Winterson*, 81.
17 Winterson, *Sexing*, 14.
18 Julia Kristeva, *In the Beginning Was Love: Psychoanalysis and Faith*, trans. Arthur Goldhammer (New York: Columbia University Press, 1987), 5.
19 Ibid., 24.
20 Ibid.
21 Ibid.
22 Ibid.
23 Ibid., 25.
24 See Freud's *The Future of an Illusion* for his most fully fleshed thoughts on religion, which are complicated and ambivalent, seeing religion simultaneously as a civilizing force and an illusion that an enlightened atheism inevitably will shed. Sigmund Freud, *The Future of an Illusion*, trans. J.A. Underwood and Shaun Whiteside (London: Penguin, 2004).
25 Kristeva, *Beginning*, 42.
26 Ibid.
27 Ibid.

28 Here Kristeva is moving on somewhat from Freud's thought on Christianity in *Totem and Taboo*, which sees the 'original sin' of Christianity as the usurping of the father's position as God by the son – an Oedipal drama quite different from Kristeva's maternal imagining. Sigmund Freud, *Totem and Taboo: Some Points of Agreement Between the Mental Lives of Savages and Neurotics*, trans. James Strachey (London and New York: Routledge, 2001).

29 Winterson, *Sexing*, 4.

30 Ibid.

31 The prophet referred to here is Hosea, who wrote 'out of Egypt I called my son' (Hos. 11:1 (New International Version)). This type of retrofitting of Christian narrative in relation to Jewish prophecy is common in the New Testament.

32 Winterson, *Sexing*, 32.

33 Ibid.

34 Ibid.

35 Ibid.

36 Ibid., 33.

37 Marcella Althaus-Reid, *Indecent Theology: Theological Perversions in Sex, Gender and Politics* (London and New York: Routledge, 2000), 48.

38 Elizabeth Johnson, *Truly Our Sister: A Theology in the Communion of Saints* (New York and London: Continuum, 2003), 7.

39 Althaus-Reid, *Indecent Theology*, 67.

40 Ibid., 69.

41 Winterson, *Sexing*, 32.

42 Jeffrey Roessner, 'Writing a History of Difference: Jeanette Winterson's "Sexing the Cherry" and Angela Carter's "Wise Children"', *College Literature* 29.1 (2002): 107.

43 Winterson, *Sexing*, 22.

44 Ibid., 70.

45 Ibid.

46 Paulina Palmer, '*The Passion*: Storytelling, Fantasy, Desire', *'I'm Telling You Stories': Jeanette Winterson and the Politics of Reading*, ed. Helena Grice and Tim Woods (Amsterdam: Rodopi, 1998), 110.

Chapter 5

1. Jeanette Winterson, *Written on the Body* (London: Vintage, 1992).
2. Brian Finney, 'Bonded by Language: Jeanette Winterson's *Written on the Body*', *Women and Language* 25.2 (2002): 25.
3. Marcella Althaus-Reid, *Indecent Theology: Theological Perversions in Sex, Gender and Politics* (London and New York: Routledge, 2000).
4. Marcella Althaus-Reid, *The Queer God* (London and New York: Routledge, 2003), 43.
5. Meister Eckhart cited in Chris Boesel and Catherine Keller, eds, 'Introduction', *Apophatic Bodies: Negative Theology, Incarnation, and Relationality* (New York: Fordham University Press, 2009), 1.
6. See, for instance, Jacques Derrida's 'How to Avoid Speaking: Denials', *Derrida and Negative Theology*, ed. Harold Coward and Toby Foshay (Albany: State University of New York Press, 1992).
7. Catherine Keller, 'The Apophasis of Gender: A Fourfold Unsaying of Feminist Theology', *Journal of the Academy of American Religion* 76.4 (2008): 905–933. Keller expands her thoughts on negative theology in *Cloud of the Impossible: Negative Theology and Planetary Engagement* (New York: Columbia University Press, 2015).
8. Kevin Hart, *Trespass of the Sign: Deconstruction, Theology and Philosophy* (Cambridge: Cambridge University Press, 1989).
9. Nicholas of Cusa cited in Boesel and Keller, 'Introduction', 5.
10. Keller, 'Apophasis', 910.
11. Ibid., 908.
12. Nicholas of Cusa, *On God as Not-Other: A Translation and an Appraisal of De Lil Non Aliud*, trans. Jasper Hopkins (Minneapolis: University of Minnesota Press, 1979), 109.
13. Derrida, 'How to Avoid', 77.
14. Many cultures, for instance, Maori and Samoan societies, have other third sex/gender positions; however, sociologist M. Morgan Holmes has warned against uncritical utopian valorization of these systems, pointing out that the existence of third categories of self does not suggest a valuing of sex/gender variance. M. Morgan Holmes,

'Locating Third Sexes', *Transformations* 8 (2004), http://www.transformationsjournal.org/journal/issue_08/article_03.shtml.

15. Judith Butler, *Gender Trouble: Feminism and the Subversion of Identity* (New York and London: Routledge, 2006), 33.

16. Lauren Berlant, for instance, points out that in-utero photography of foetuses is used by anti-abortion activists to 'humanize' foetuses through gendering – no longer the inhuman 'it', foetuses are subjectified as 'he' or 'she'. Lauren Berlant, *The Queen of America Goes to Washington City* (Durham: Duke University Press, 1997).

17. Viviane K. Namaste, *Invisible Lives: The Erasure of Transsexual and Transgendered People* (Chicago and London: Chicago University Press, 2000), 260.

18. Susannah Cornwall, 'The Kenosis of Unambiguous Sex in the Body of Christ: Intersex, Theology and Existing "For the Other"', *Theology & Sexuality* 14.2 (2008): 181.

19. I should note that some non-binary or intersex activists have lobbied successfully for legal recognition as a third sex in documents such as birth certificates. See 'Neither Man nor Woman: Norrie Wins Gender Appeal', *Sydney Morning Herald*, 2 April 2014, https://www.smh.com.au/national/nsw/neither-man-nor-woman-norrie-wins-gender-appeal-20140402-35xgt.html. While it is beyond the scope of this book to investigate the intricacies of trans and intersex activism, it is worth stating that, while gender is being remade increasingly (especially in queer and trans spaces), the binary will remain with us for some time institutionally and socially. The impossibility of a position outside the binary that we see in *Written on the Body* may well be briefly available in a few rare spaces, temporally and spatially limited.

20. Winterson, *Written*, 84.

21. Ibid., 15.

22. Ibid., 89.

23. Myfanwy McDonald, 'The Non Surgical Option: Deciding Not to Decide About Gender Identity', *Boundary Writing: An Exploration of Race, Culture and Gender Binaries in Contemporary Australia*, ed. Lynette Russell (Honolulu: Hawai'i University Press, 2003), 43.

24 See Judith (Jack) Halberstam, *Female Masculinity* (Durham: Duke University Press, 1998); and C. Jacob Hale, 'Consuming the Living, Dis(Re)Membering the Dead in the Butch/Ftm Borderlands', *GLQ* 4.2 (1998): 311–348.
25 Hale, 'Consuming the Living', 318.
26 Jennifer Hansen, 'Written on the Body, Written by the Senses', *Philosophy and Literature* 29 (2005): 367.
27 Ibid.
28 Winterson, *Written*, 73.
29 Ibid., 71.
30 Ibid., 50.
31 While historically there have been some limited alliances between heterosexual women and gay men based around shared objects of desire, such alliances between, for instance, lesbians and straight men are rare to non-existent. Moreover, alliances between trans and cis people are even rarer.
32 Derrida, 'How to Avoid', 77.
33 Ibid.
34 Eve Kosofsky Sedgwick, *Epistemology of the Closet* (Berkeley: University of California Press, 2008), 26.
35 Judith Butler, *Undoing Gender* (New York: Routledge, 2004), 80.
36 Winterson, *Written*, 67.
37 Ibid., 54.
38 John D. Caputo, 'Spectral Hermeneutics', *After the Death of God*, ed. Jeffrey Robbins (New York: Columbia University Press, 2007), 51.
39 Jean-Luc Marion, *God Without Being*, trans. Thomas A. Carlson (Chicago: University of Chicago Press, 1991), 166.
40 Ibid., 178.
41 Winterson, *Written*, 106.
42 Sedgwick, *Epistemology*, 72.
43 Jacques Derrida, *The Gift of Death*, trans. David Wills (Chicago: University of Chicago Press, 1994), 78.
44 Ibid.
45 Judith Butler, *Giving an Account of Oneself* (New York: Fordham University Press, 2005), 83.

46 Judith (Jack) Halberstam, *In a Queer Time and Place: Transgendered Bodies, Subcultural Lives* (New York and London: New York University Press, 2006), 97.

Chapter 6

1. http://www.jeanettewinterson.com/book/art-lies.
2. David Harvey, *A Brief History of Neoliberalism* (New York: Oxford University Press, 2005), 2.
3. Jonathan Crary, *24/7: Late Capitalism and the Ends of Sleep* (London and New York: Verso, 2013), 30.
4. Ibid., 40.
5. Jeanette Winterson, *Tanglewreck* (London: A&C Black, 2008), 137.
6. Harvey, *Neoliberalism*, 171.
7. Wendy Brown, *Walled States, Waning Sovereignty* (New York: Zone, 2010), 63.
8. Ibid., 64.
9. Emily McAvan, *The Postmodern Sacred: Popular Culture Spirituality in the Science Fiction, Fantasy and Urban Fantasy Genres* (Jefferson: McFarland, 2012), 5.
10. Jeanette Winterson, *Art & Lies* (New York: Alfred A. Knopf, 1995), 103.
11. Fredric Jameson, 'The Antinomies of the Postmodern', *The Cultural Turn: Selected Writings on the Postmodern, 1983–1998* (London and New York: Verso, 1998), 58.
12. Michael Hardt, 'The Common in Communism', *The Idea of Communism*, ed. Costas Douzinas and Slavoj Žižek (London and New York: Verso, 2010), 137.
13. Winterson, *Art & Lies*, 14.
14. Ibid.
15. Judith Butler, *Frames of War: When Is Life Grievable?* (London and New York: Verso, 2009), 74.
16. Winterson, *Art & Lies*, 65.

17 Susana Onega, *Jeanette Winterson* (Manchester: Manchester University Press, 2006), 143.
18 Winterson, *Art & Lies*, 65.
19 Ibid.
20 Ibid., 8.
21 Slavoj Žižek, *The Year of Living Dangerously* (New York: Verso, 2012), 48.
22 Winterson, *Art & Lies*, 43.
23 Sara Ahmed, *The Cultural Politics of Emotion* (New York: Routledge, 2004), 45.
24 Winterson, *Art & Lies*, 160.
25 Ibid., 82.
26 Ibid., 83.
27 Ibid., 13.
28 Ibid., 15.
29 Ibid., 13.
30 Michel Foucault, *The History of Sexuality. Volume Three: The Care of the Self*, trans. Robert Hurley (London: Penguin, 1986), 48.
31 Winterson, *Art & Lies*, 39.
32 Winterson, *Art Objects*, 4.
33 Winterson, *Art & Lies*, 47.
34 Christy Burns, 'Fantastic Language: Winterson's Recovery of the Postmodern Word', *Contemporary Literature* 37.2 (1996): 388.
35 Winterson, *Art Objects*, 153.
36 Winterson, *Art & Lies*, 55.
37 John D. Caputo, *The Weakness of God* (Indianapolis: Indiana University Press, 2006), 104.
38 Winterson, *Art & Lies*, 51.
39 Ibid., 55.
40 Ibid., 13.
41 Sonya Andermahr, *Jeanette Winterson* (Hampshire: Palgrave MacMillan, 2009), 95.
42 Vincent Francone, 'An Interview with Jeanette Winterson', *Rain Taxi* (2005), http://www.raintaxi.com/an-interview-with-jeanette-winterson.

Chapter 7

1. In *Written on the Body*, Louise's husband Elgin is Jewish, but there is more textual interest in his sexual life than his religious one. (Jeanette Winterson, *Written on the Body* (London: Vintage, 1992).) Judaism is the other of Christianity in Winterson's worlds – there are no Hindus, Buddhists or Muslims, only Christians and Jews.
2. Helena Grice and Tim Woods, 'Grand (Dis)unified Theories? Dislocated Discourses in Gut Symmetries', *'I'm Telling You Stories': Jeanette Winterson and the Politics of Reading*, ed. Helena Grice and Tim Woods (Amsterdam: Rodopi, 1998), 118.
3. Jeanette Winterson, *Gut Symmetries* (New York: Alfred A. Knopf, 1997), 162.
4. Susana Onega, *Jeanette Winterson* (Manchester: Manchester University Press, 2006), 159.
5. Winterson, *Gut Symmetries*, 85.
6. Ibid., 4.
7. Grice and Woods, 'Grand (Dis)unified Theories', 120.
8. Winterson, *Gut Symmetries*, 195.
9. Ibid., 100.
10. Ibid., 9.
11. Ibid., 171.
12. Jeanette Winterson, *The Passion* (New York: Grove, 1987), 68.
13. The novel makes reference to this ambivalence about Stella's identity, by suggesting that her mother does not see her daughter as Jewish. 'Her daughter was not Jewish. Jewishness is continued through the female line. Mama would not have her daughter given up to Papa's passion.' Ibid., 114.
14. Ibid., 131.
15. Gershom Scholem, *Major Trends in Jewish Mysticism* (New York: Schocken, 1995), 17.
16. Winterson, *Gut Symmetries*, 44.
17. Ibid., 48.
18. Scholem, *Major Trends*, 17.

19 Winterson, *Gut Symmetries*, 78.
20 Kenneth Seeskin, 'Maimonides', *The Stanford Encyclopedia of Philosophy*, ed. Edward N. Zalta (2017), https://plato.stanford.edu/archives/spr2017/entries/maimonides, 1.59.
21 Ibid., 1.54 [italics in the original].
22 Ibid., https://plato.stanford.edu/entries/maimonides/#GodViaNeg.
23 *Tzimtzum* also may be considered somewhat analogous to the Christian idea of kenosis, the 'weakening' of God, which has been a persistent theme of the post-structuralist influenced theory and theology of the last twenty years. Notable examples of this can be found in Gianni Vattimo's book *Belief*, and John Caputo's *The Weakness of God*. See Gianni Vattimo, *Belief*, trans. Luca D'Isanto (Stanford: Stanford University Press, 1999) and John D. Caputo, *The Weakness of God* (Indianapolis: Indiana University Press, 2006).
24 For a sense of the debate, see excerpts of kabbalistic thought in the Alan Unterman edited collection *The Kabbalistic Tradition*. Unterman notes that Chaim Vital, disciple of noted kabbalist Isaac Luria, argues for the strictly metaphorical interpretation of *tzimtzum*, saying 'we cannot use any images or forms at all, heaven forbid, except when to make matters intelligible we need to speak using parables and images'. By contrast, kabbalist Emanuel Chai Ricchi argues that 'a person who is careful about the honour of his Creator needs to take the idea of the Divine Contract [*tzimtzum*] in a literal manner. He will thus avoid any blemish to God's honour in thinking that His essence is also to be found among lowly physical things.' Alan Unterman, ed., *The Kabbalistic Tradition*, trans. Alan Unterman (London: Penguin, 2008), 4, 7.
25 Arthur Green, *Radical Judaism: Rethinking God and Tradition* (New Haven and London: Yale University Press, 2010), 19.
26 Scholem, *Major Trends*, 17.
27 Winterson, *Gut Symmetries*, 85.
28 Ibid., 172.
29 Chaim Vital cited in Unterman, *Kabbalistic Tradition*, 142.
30 Winterson, *Gut Symmetries*, 95.
31 Ibid., 100.

32. Ibid., 103.
33. Michel de Certeau, *The Mystic Fable. Volume One: The Sixteenth and Seventeenth Centuries*, trans. Michael B. Smith (Chicago and London: University of Chicago Press, 1992), 13.
34. Michel de Certeau, 'Mysticism', trans. Marsanne Bremer, *Diacritics* 22.2 (1992): 14.
35. Ibid., 15.
36. Jacques Derrida, 'How to Avoid Speaking: Denials', *Derrida and Negative Theology*, ed. Harold Coward and Toby Foshay (Albany: State University of New York Press, 1992), 77.
37. Winterson, *Gut Symmetries*, 75.
38. Onega, *Jeanette Winterson*, 168.
39. Winterson, *Gut Symmetries*, 83.
40. Ibid., 171.
41. Richard Kearney, *Anatheism: Returning to God After God* (New York: Columbia University Press, 2011), 102.
42. Winterson, *Gut Symmetries*, 72.
43. Ibid., 73.
44. Mary Holland, *Succeeding Postmodernism: Language and Humanism in Contemporary American Literature* (New York and London: Bloomsbury, 2013).
45. Ibid., 216.

Chapter 8

1. Jeanette Winterson, *The PowerBook* (New York: Vintage, 2000), 30.
2. Elaine Showalter, 'Eternal Triangles', *Guardian* (2000), https://www.theguardian.com/books/2000/sep/02/fiction.jeanettewinterson1.
3. Jean Baudrillard, *Simulacra and Simulation*, trans. Sheila Faria Glaser (Ann Arbor: University of Michigan, 1994), 1.
4. Alan Kirby, *Digimodernism: How New Technologies Dismantle the Postmodern and Reconfigure Our Culture* (New York and London: Continuum, 2009), 123.

5 Winterson, *PowerBook*, 4.
6 Sonya Andermahr, *Jeanette Winterson* (Hampshire: Palgrave MacMillan, 2009), 108.
7 Winterson, *PowerBook*, 5.
8 N. Katherine Hayles, *How We Became Posthuman* (Chicago: University of Chicago Press, 1999), 3.
9 Winterson, *PowerBook*, 108.
10 Andermahr, *Jeanette Winterson*, 108.
11 Winterson, *PowerBook*, 73.
12 Ibid., 30.
13 Judith (Jack) Halberstam, *In a Queer Time and Place: Transgendered Bodies, Subcultural Lives* (New York and London: New York University Press, 2006), 54.
14 Winterson, *PowerBook*, 25.
15 Ibid., 29.
16 Gavin Keulks, 'Winterson's Recent Work: Navigating Realism and Postmodernism', *Jeanette Winterson: A Contemporary Critical Guide*, ed. Sonya Andermahr (London and New York: Continuum, 2009), 150.
17 Mary Holland, *Succeeding Postmodernism: Language and Humanism in Contemporary American Literature* (New York and London: Bloomsbury, 2013).
18 Mark C. Taylor, *About Religion: Economies of Faith in Virtual Culture* (Chicago: University of Chicago Press, 1999), 2.
19 Ibid., 21.
20 Ibid., 5.
21 Ibid., 46.
22 Winterson, *PowerBook*, 63.
23 Ibid., 166.
24 Jurgen Moltmann, *God in Creation: A New Theology of Creation and the Spirit of God*, trans. Margaret Kohl (Minneapolis: Fortress, 1993), 88.
25 Winterson, *PowerBook*, 74.
26 Ibid., 120.

27 John A. McClure, *Partial Faiths: Postsecular Fiction in the Age of Pynchon and Morrison* (Athens and London: University of Georgia Press, 2007), ix.
28 Winterson, *PowerBook*, 119.
29 Ibid.
30 Usage of this term taken from Richard Kearney, *Anatheism: Returning to God After God* (New York: Columbia University Press, 2011).
31 Winterson, *PowerBook*, 4.
32 Ibid., 204.
33 Ibid., 223.
34 Sigmund Freud, *An Outline of Psychoanalysis*, trans. James Strachey (New York and London: W.W. Norton, 1989), 18–19.
35 Winterson, *PowerBook*, 272.
36 John D. Caputo, *The Prayers and Tears of Jacques Derrida: Religion Without Religion* (Indianapolis: Indiana University Press, 1997), xix.
37 Winterson, *PowerBook*, 169.
38 Ibid., 89.
39 Ibid., 151.
40 Ibid., 152.
41 Ibid.
42 Ibid., 141.
43 Jacques Derrida, *The Gift of Death*, trans. David Wills (Chicago: University of Chicago Press, 1994), 41.
44 Winterson, *PowerBook*, 237.
45 Ibid.
46 Ibid., 267.
47 Ibid., 288.
48 Keulks, 'Winterson's Recent Work', 150.
49 Winterson, *PowerBook*, 267.
50 Ibid., 95.
51 Ibid., 141.
52 Jeanette Winterson, *Oranges Are Not the Only Fruit* (New York: Atlantic, 1985), 170.
53 Interestingly, Winterson makes reference to 'two Buddhists in saffron robes [who] were chanting and dancing in front of a portable shrine'

(*PowerBook*, 272). Ali's lover tells her: 'be here now' (ibid.). This is a rare reference to an Eastern religion beyond the Christian and Jewish textual traditions that sustain Winterson's writing. It is significant, I think, that it comes at the end of a narrative about cyberspace, which is after all about flow – a fluid form of identity and practice that has some resonance with Buddhist ideas. This would be rather a different model of relating to otherness than we more usually see in Winterson's post-Christian motifs.

54 Winterson, *PowerBook*, 242.
55 Ibid., 289.

Chapter 9

1 Susana Onega, *Jeanette Winterson* (Manchester: Manchester University Press, 2006), 8.
2 Ibid., 205.
3 Jeanette Winterson, *Lighthousekeeping* (Orlando: Harcourt, 2004).
4 Gavin Keulks, 'Winterson's Recent Work: Navigating Realism and Postmodernism', *Jeanette Winterson: A Contemporary Critical Guide*, ed. Sonya Andermahr (London and New York: Continuum, 2009), 151.
5 *JPS Hebrew-English Tanakh* (Philadelphia: Jewish Publication Society, 2003).
6 Winterson, *Lighthousekeeping*, 57.
7 Ibid., 49.
8 Ibid., 139.
9 Keulks, 'Winterson's Recent Work', 153.
10 Northrop Frye, *The Great Code: The Bible and Literature* (San Diego: Harcourt, 1982).
11 Winterson, *Lighthousekeeping*, 40.
12 Ibid., 41.
13 Ibid., 135.
14 Ibid., 107.
15 Ibid.
16 Onega, *Jeanette Winterson*, 219.

17 Winterson, *Lighthousekeeping*, 57.
18 Ibid., 102.
19 Ibid., 26.
20 Ibid., 27.
21 Ibid., 54.
22 Richard Kearney, *Anatheism: Returning to God After God* (New York: Columbia University Press, 2011).
23 Winterson, *Lighthousekeeping*, 120.
24 Ibid., 166.
25 Richard Kearney, *Anatheism: Returning to God After God* (New York: Columbia University Press, 2011), 5.
26 Winterson, *Lighthousekeeping*, 183.
27 Sonya Andermahr, *Jeanette Winterson* (Hampshire: Palgrave MacMillan, 2009), 118.
28 Winterson, *Lighthousekeeping*, 170.
29 Ibid.
30 Ibid., 121.
31 W.H. Auden cited in Kearney, *Anatheism*, 15.
32 Richard Kearney and Jens Zimmerman, *Reimagining the Sacred: Richard Kearney Debates God* (New York: Columbia University Press, 2016), 32.
33 Catherine Keller, *Face of the Deep: A Theology of Becoming* (London and New York: Routledge, 2003).
34 Sigmund Freud, *Civilization and its Discontents*, trans. James Strachey (New York: Norton, 1961), 19.
35 Julia Kristeva, *This Incredible Need to Believe*, trans. Beverley Bie Brahic (New York: Columbia University Press, 2011), 7.
36 Ibid.
37 Kearney and Zimmerman, *Reimagining*, 29.
38 Winterson, *Lighthousekeeping*, 88.
39 Ibid., 187.
40 Ibid.
41 Ibid., 188.
42 Ibid., 161.

43 Ibid., 85.
44 Ibid., 90.
45 Judith Butler, *Gender Trouble: Feminism and the Subversion of Identity* (New York and London: Routledge, 2006).
46 Keulks, 'Winterson's Recent Work', 154.
47 Mircea Eliade, *The Sacred and the Profane: The Nature of Religion*, trans. Willard Trask (Orlando: Harcourt, 1959).
48 Winterson, *Lighthousekeeping*, 92.
49 John A. McClure, *Partial Faiths: Postsecular Fiction in the Age of Pynchon and Morrison* (Athens and London: University of Georgia Press, 2007), ix.
50 John D. Caputo, *The Weakness of God* (Indianapolis: Indiana University Press, 2006), 4.
51 Winterson, *Lighthousekeeping*, 187.
52 Ibid., 127.
53 Ibid., 167.
54 Ibid., 134.

Chapter 10

1 Darko Suvin, *Metamorphoses of Science Fiction* (New Haven and London: Yale University Press, 1979), 4.
2 Amitav Ghosh, *The Great Derangement: Climate Change and the Unthinkable* (Chicago: University of Chicago Press, 2017).
3 Timothy Morton, 'Ecology Without the Present', *Oxford Literary Review* 34.2 (2012): 231.
4 Jeanette Winterson, *The Stone Gods* (London: Penguin, 2007), 8.
5 Ibid., 47.
6 Winterson, *Stone Gods*, 38.
7 Cited in Susana Onega, 'The Trauma Paradigm and the Ethics of Affect in Jeanette Winterson's *The Stone Gods*', *Ethics and Trauma in Contemporary British Fiction*, ed. Susana Onega and Jean-Michel Ganteau (Amsterdam: Rodopi, 2011), 275.

8. Catherine Keller, *Apocalypse Now and Then: A Feminist Guide to the End of the World* (Minneapolis: Fortress, 1996), 13.
9. Jeanette Winterson, *The Passion* (New York: Grove, 1987), 91.
10. Keller, *Apocalypse*, 75.
11. Winterson, *Stone Gods*, 13.
12. Ibid., 28.
13. Luna Dolezal, 'The Body, Gender and Biotechnology in Jeanette Winterson's *The Stone Gods*', *Literature and Medicine* 33.1 (2015): 91.
14. Winterson, *Stone Gods*, 21.
15. Ibid., 23.
16. Ibid., 38.
17. Jason W. Moore, *Capitalism in the Web of Life: Ecology and the Accumulation of Capital* (New York: Verso, 2015), 2.
18. Ibid., 29.
19. Winterson, *Stone Gods*, 133.
20. Mircea Eliade, *The Sacred and the Profane: The Nature of Religion*, trans. Willard Trask (Orlando: Harcourt, 1959), 34.
21. Winterson, *Stone Gods*, 131.
22. Ibid., 132.
23. Keller, *Apocalypse*, 42.
24. Winterson, *Stone Gods*, 9.
25. Ibid., 13.
26. Ibid., 111.
27. Ibid., 7.
28. Ibid., 109.
29. Ibid., 112.
30. Ibid., 89.
31. Ibid., 99.
32. Onega, 'Trauma Paradigm', 296.
33. Alain Badiou, with Nicholas Truong, *In Praise of Love*, trans. Peter Bush (London: Serpent's Tail, 2012), 26.
34. Winterson, *Stone Gods*, 111.
35. Ibid., 136.
36. Ibid., 111.

37 Ibid., 179.
38 Ibid., 207.
39 Catherine Keller, *God and Power: Counter-Apocalyptic Journeys* (Minneapolis: Fortress, 2005), 57.
40 Keller, *Apocalypse*, 68.
41 Dolezal, 'Body', 93.
42 Winterson, *Stone Gods*, 132.
43 Ibid., 153.
44 Onega, 'Trauma Paradigm', 278.
45 Sigmund Freud, *Beyond the Pleasure Principle and Other Writings*, trans. John Reddick (London and New York: Penguin, 2003).
46 Nicola M. Merola, 'Materializing a Geotraumatic and Melancholy Anthropocene: Jeanette Winterson's *The Stone Gods*', *Minnesota Review* 83 (2014): 130.
47 Winterson, *Stone Gods*, 105.
48 Keller, *Apocalypse*, 30.
49 Ibid., 73.

Conclusion

1 Bill Moyers, Jeanette Winterson and Will Power, 'Bill Moyers on Faith and Reason', PBS (2006), https://www.pbs.org/moyers/faithandreason/print/faithandreason103_print.html.
2 Mark C. Taylor, *Erring: A Postmodern A/theology* (Chicago and London: University of Chicago Press, 1984).
3 Richard Kearney, *Anatheism: Returning to God After God* (New York: Columbia University Press, 2011).
4 Ibid.
5 Moyers, Winterson and Power, 'Bill Moyers on Faith and Reason'.
6 Jeanette Winterson, *Art & Lies: A Piece for Three Voices and a Bawd* (New York: Alfred A. Knopf, 1995), 13.
7 Sara Ahmed, *Queer Phenomenology* (Durham and London: Duke University Press, 2006), 1.

8   Moyers, Winterson and Power, 'Bill Moyers on Faith and Reason'.
9   Jeanette Winterson, *The Passion* (New York: Grove, 1987), 27.
10 Alain Badiou, with Nicholas Truong, *In Praise of Love*, trans. Peter Bush (London: Serpent's Tail, 2012).
11 John D. Caputo, *The Weakness of God* (Indianapolis: Indiana University Press, 2006), 292.
12 Amy Hungerford, *Postmodern Belief: American Literature and Religion Since 1960* (Princeton and Oxford: Princeton University Press, 2010) and John A. McClure, *Partial Faiths: Postsecular Fiction in the Age of Pynchon and Morrison* (Athens and London: University of Georgia Press, 2007).

Bibliography

Jeanette Winterson, *Oranges Are Not the Only Fruit* (New York: Atlantic, 1985).
Jeanette Winterson, *The Passion* (New York: Grove, 1987).
Jeanette Winterson, *Sexing the Cherry* (New York: Grove, 1989).
Jeanette Winterson, *Boating for Beginners* (London: Minerva, 1990).
Jeanette Winterson, *Written on the Body* (London: Vintage, 1992).
Jeanette Winterson, *Art & Lies: A Piece for Three Voices and a Bawd* (New York: Alfred A. Knopf, 1995).
Jeanette Winterson, *Art Objects* (London and Sydney: Vintage, 1996).
Jeanette Winterson, *Gut Symmetries* (New York and London: Alfred A. Knopf, 1997).
Jeanette Winterson, *The PowerBook* (New York: Vintage, 2000).
Jeanette Winterson, *Lighthousekeeping* (Orlando: Harcourt, 2004).
Jeanette Winterson, *The Stone Gods* (London: Penguin, 2007).
Jeanette Winterson, *Tanglewreck* (London: A&C Black, 2008).
Jeanette Winterson, *Why Be Happy When You Could Be Normal?* (London: Jonathan Cape, 2011).
Jeanette Winterson, *The Daylight Gate* (London: Arrow, 2012).
Jeanette Winterson, *The Gap of Time* (London: Hogarth, 2015).

Works Cited

Sara Ahmed, *The Cultural Politics of Emotion* (New York: Routledge, 2004).
Sara Ahmed, *Queer Phenomenology* (Durham and London: Duke University Press, 2006).
Marcella Althaus-Reid, *Indecent Theology: Theological Perversions in Sex, Gender and Politics* (London and New York: Routledge, 2000).
Marcella Althaus-Reid, *The Queer God* (London and New York: Routledge, 2003).

Sonya Andermahr, 'Reinventing the Romance', *Jeanette Winterson: A Contemporary Critical Guide*, ed. Sonya Andermahr (London and New York: Continuum, 2007), 82–99.

Sonya Andermahr, *Jeanette Winterson* (Hampshire: Palgrave MacMillan, 2009).

Saint Augustine, *Confessions* (London: Penguin, 1961).

Alain Badiou, *Ethics: An Essay on the Understanding of Evil*, trans. Peter Hallward (New York: Verso, 2001).

Alain Badiou, *Saint Paul: The Foundation of Universalism*, trans. Ray Brassier (Stanford: Stanford University Press, 2003).

Alain Badiou, *The Century*, trans. Alberto Toscano (Cambridge: Polity, 2007).

Alain Badiou, with Nicholas Truong, *In Praise of Love*, trans. Peter Bush (London: Serpent's Tail, 2012).

Roland Barthes, *A Lover's Discourse: Fragments*, trans. Richard Howard (London: Vintage, 2002).

Jean Baudrillard, *Simulacra and Simulation*, trans. Sheila Faria Glaser (Ann Arbor: University of Michigan, 1994).

Zygmunt Bauman, *Liquid Modernity* (Hoboken: Wiley, 2013).

Ulrich Beck and Elisabeth Beck-Gernsheim, *Individualization: Institutionalized Individualism and its Social and Political Consequences* (London: Sage, 2001).

Lauren Berlant, *The Queen of America Goes to Washington City* (Durham: Duke University Press, 1997).

Chris Boesel and Catherine Keller, eds, 'Introduction', *Apophatic Bodies: Negative Theology, Incarnation, and Relationality* (New York: Fordham University Press, 2009), 1–24.

Wendy Brown, *Regulating Aversion: Tolerance in the Age of Identity and Empire* (Princeton and Oxford: Princeton University Press, 2006).

Wendy Brown, *Walled States, Waning Sovereignty* (New York: Zone, 2010).

Christy Burns, 'Fantastic Language: Winterson's Recovery of the Postmodern Word', *Contemporary Literature* 37.2 (1996): 278–306.

Judith Butler, *Undoing Gender* (New York: Routledge, 2004).

Judith Butler, *Giving an Account of Oneself* (New York: Fordham University Press, 2005).

Judith Butler, *Gender Trouble: Feminism and the Subversion of Identity* (New York and London: Routledge, 2006).

Judith Butler, *Frames of War: When is Life Grievable?* (London and New York: Verso, 2009).

John D. Caputo, *The Prayers and Tears of Jacques Derrida: Religion Without Religion* (Indianapolis: Indiana University Press, 1997).

John D. Caputo, *The Weakness of God* (Indianapolis: Indiana University Press, 2006).

John D. Caputo, 'Spectral Hermeneutics', *After the Death of God*, ed. Jeffrey Robbins (New York: Columbia University Press, 2007), 47–88.

Michel de Certeau, *The Mystic Fable. Volume One: The Sixteenth and Seventeenth Centuries*, trans. Michael B. Smith (Chicago and London: University of Chicago Press, 1992).

Michel de Certeau, 'Mysticism', trans. Marsanne Bremer, *Diacritics* 22.2 (1992): 11–26.

Helene Cixous, 'The Laugh of the Medusa', *Signs* 1.4 (Summer 1976): 875–893.

Jeffrey Jerome Cohen, 'Monster Culture: Seven Theses', *Monster Theory: Reading Culture*, ed. Jeffrey Jerome Cohen (Minneapolis and London: University of Minnesota Press, 1996), 3–25.

Susannah Cornwall, 'The Kenosis of Unambiguous Sex in the Body of Christ: Intersex, Theology and Existing "For the Other"', *Theology & Sexuality* 14.2 (2008): 181–199.

Jonathan Crary, *24/7: Late Capitalism and the Ends of Sleep* (London and New York: Verso, 2013).

Barbara Creed, *The Monstrous-Feminine: Film, Feminism and Psychoanalysis* (London and New York: Routledge, 1993).

Nicholas of Cusa, *On God as Not-Other: A Translation and an Appraisal of De Lil Non Aliud*, trans. Jasper Hopkins (Minneapolis: University of Minnesota Press, 1979).

Gilles Deleuze, *The Logic of Sense*, trans. Mark Lester and Charles Stivale (London and New York: Continuum, 2004).

Michelle Denby, 'Religion and Spirituality', *A Contemporary Critical Guide: Jeanette Winterson*, ed. Sonya Andermahr (London and New York: Continuum, 2007), 100–113.

Jacques Derrida, *Of Grammatology*, trans. Gayatri Chakravorty Spivak (Baltimore: Johns Hopkins University Press, 1976).

Jacques Derrida, 'How to Avoid Speaking: Denials', *Derrida and Negative Theology*, ed. Harold Coward and Toby Foshay (Albany: State University of New York Press, 1992), 73–142.

Jacques Derrida, *The Gift of Death*, trans. David Wills (Chicago: University of Chicago Press, 1994).

Jacques Derrida, *Writing and Difference*, trans. Alan Bass (New York and London: Routledge, 2001).

Laura Doan, ed., *The Lesbian Postmodern* (New York: Columbia University Press, 1994).

Luna Dolezal, 'The Body, Gender and Biotechnology in Jeanette Winterson's *The Stone Gods*', *Literature and Medicine* 33.1 (2015): 91–112.

Terry Eagleton, *Culture and the Death of God* (New Haven and London: Yale University Press, 2014).

Mircea Eliade, *The Sacred and the Profane: The Nature of Religion*, trans. Willard Trask (Orlando: Harcourt, 1959).

Brian Finney, 'Bonded by Language: Jeanette Winterson's *Written on the Body*', *Women and Language* 25.2 (2002): 23–46.

Michel Foucault, *The History of Sexuality. Volume Three: The Care of the Self*, trans. Robert Hurley (London: Penguin, 1986).

Michel Foucault, *The Will to Knowledge: The History of Sexuality*, trans. Robert Hurley (London: Penguin, 1990).

Michel Foucault, *The History of Sexuality. Volume One: The Will to Knowledge*, trans. Robert Hurley (London, Penguin: 1998).

Sigmund Freud, *Civilization and its Discontents*, trans. James Strachey (New York: Norton, 1961).

Sigmund Freud, *An Outline of Psychoanalysis*, trans. James Strachey (New York and London: W.W. Norton, 1989).

Sigmund Freud, *Totem and Taboo: Some Points of Agreement Between the Mental Lives of Savages and Neurotics*, trans. James Strachey (London and New York: Routledge, 2001).

Sigmund Freud, *Beyond the Pleasure Principle and Other Writings*, trans. John Reddick (London and New York: Penguin, 2003).

Sigmund Freud, *The Future of an Illusion*, trans. J.A. Underwood and Shaun Whiteside (London: Penguin, 2004).

Northrop Frye, *The Great Code: The Bible and Literature* (San Diego: Harcourt, 1982).

Amitav Ghosh, *The Great Derangement: Climate Change and the Unthinkable* (Chicago: University of Chicago Press, 2017).

Anthony Giddens, *The Transformation of Intimacy: Sexuality, Love and Eroticism in Modern Societies* (Cambridge: Polity, 1992).

Arthur Green, *Radical Judaism: Rethinking God and Tradition* (New Haven and London: Yale University Press, 2010).

Helena Grice and Tim Woods, 'Grand (Dis)unified Theories? Dislocated Discourses in Gut Symmetries', *'I'm Telling You Stories': Jeanette Winterson and the Politics of Reading*, ed. Helena Grice and Tim Woods (Amsterdam: Rodopi, 1998), 117–126.

Helena Grice and Tim Woods, 'Winterson's Dislocated Discourses', *Jeanette Winterson*, ed. Sonya Andermahr (London: Continuum, 2007), 27–41.

Jennifer Gustar, 'Language and the Limits of Desire', *Jeanette Winterson: A Contemporary Critical Guide*, ed. Sonya Andermahr (London and New York: Continuum, 2007), 55–68.

Judith (Jack) Halberstam, *Female Masculinity* (Durham: Duke University Press, 1998).

Judith (Jack) Halberstam, *In a Queer Time and Place: Transgendered Bodies, Subcultural Lives* (New York and London: New York University Press, 2006).

C. Jacob Hale, 'Consuming the Living, Dis(Re)Membering the Dead in the Butch/Ftm Borderlands', *GLQ* 4.2 (1998): 311–348.

Jennifer Hansen, 'Written on the Body, Written by the Senses', *Philosophy and Literature* 29 (2005): 365–378.

Michael Hardt, 'The Common in Communism', *The Idea of Communism*, ed. Costas Douzinas and Slavoj Žižek (London and New York: Verso, 2010).

Kevin Hart, *Trespass of the Sign: Deconstruction, Theology and Philosophy* (Cambridge: Cambridge University Press, 1989).

David Harvey, *A Brief History of Neoliberalism* (New York: Oxford University Press, 2005).

Jane Haslett, 'Winterson's Fabulous Bodies', *Jeanette Winterson: A Contemporary Critical Guide*, ed. Sonya Andermahr (London and New York: Continuum, 2007), 41–54.

N. Katherine Hayles, *How We Became Posthuman* (Chicago: University of Chicago Press, 1999).

Abraham Joshua Heschel, *The Prophets* (New York: Harper Perennial, 2001).

Mary Holland, *Succeeding Postmodernism: Language and Humanism in Contemporary American Literature* (New York and London: Bloomsbury, 2013).

Amy Hungerford, *Postmodern Belief: American Literature and Religion Since 1960* (Princeton and Oxford: Princeton University Press, 2010).

Luce Irigaray, *Marine Lover of Friedrich Nietzsche*, trans. Gillian C. Gill (New York and London: Columbia University Press, 1991).

Fredric Jameson, 'The Antinomies of the Postmodern', *The Cultural Turn: Selected Writings on the Postmodern, 1983-1998* (London and New York: Verso, 1998), 50–72.

Elizabeth Johnson, *Truly Our Sister: A Theology in the Communion of Saints* (New York and London: Continuum, 2003).

Richard Kearney, *The God Who May Be: A Hermeneutics of Religion* (Bloomington: Indiana University Press, 2001).

Richard Kearney, *Anatheism: Returning to God After God* (New York: Columbia University Press, 2011).

Richard Kearney and Jens Zimmerman, *Reimagining the Sacred: Richard Kearney Debates God* (New York: Columbia University Press, 2016).

Catherine Keller, *Apocalypse Now and Then: A Feminist Guide to the End of the World* (Minneapolis: Fortress, 1996).

Catherine Keller, *Face of the Deep: A Theology of Becoming* (London and New York: Routledge, 2003).

Catherine Keller, *God and Power: Counter-Apocalyptic Journeys* (Minneapolis: Fortress, 2005).

Catherine Keller, 'The Apophasis of Gender: A Fourfold Unsaying of Feminist Theology', *Journal of the Academy of American Religion* 76.4 (2008): 905–933.

Catherine Keller, *Cloud of the Impossible: Negative Theology and Planetary Engagement* (New York: Columbia University Press, 2015).

Gavin Keulks, 'Winterson's Recent Work: Navigating Realism and Postmodernism', *Jeanette Winterson: A Contemporary Critical Guide*, ed Sonya Andermahr (London and New York: Continuum, 2009), 146–162.

Soren Kierkegaard, *Fear and Trembling: Dialectical Lyric by Johannes de Silentio*, trans. Alistair Hannay (London: Penguin, 1985).

Alan Kirby, *Digimodernism: How New Technologies Dismantle the Postmodern and Reconfigure our Culture* (New York and London: Continuum, 2009).

Julia Kristeva, *Powers of Horror: An Essay on Abjection*, trans. Leon S. Roudiez (New York: Columbia University Press, 1982).

Julia Kristeva, *In the Beginning was Love: Psychoanalysis and Faith*, trans. Arthur Goldhammer (New York: Columbia University Press, 1987).

Julia Kristeva, *This Incredible Need to Believe*, trans. Beverley Bie Brahic (New York: Columbia University Press, 2011).

Emmanuel Levinas, *Otherwise Than Being: Or Beyond Essence*, trans. Alphonso Lingis (Pittsburgh: Duquesne University Press, 1998).

Jean-Luc Marion, *God Without Being*, trans. Thomas A. Carlson (Chicago: University of Chicago Press, 1991).

Sara Martin, 'The Power of Monstrous Women: Fay Weldon's *The Life and Loves of a She-Devil* (1983), Angela Carter's *Nights at the Circus* (1984) and Jeanette Winterson's *Sexing the Cherry* (1989)', *Journal of Gender Studies* 8.2 (1999): 193–210.

Emily McAvan, *The Postmodern Sacred: Popular Culture Spirituality in the Science Fiction, Fantasy and Urban Fantasy Genres* (Jefferson: McFarland, 2012).

John A. McClure, *Partial Faiths: Postsecular Fiction in the Age of Pynchon and Morrison* (Athens and London: University of Georgia Press, 2007).

Myfanwy McDonald, 'The Non Surgical Option: Deciding Not to Decide About Gender Identity', *Boundary Writing: An Exploration of Race, Culture and Gender Binaries in Contemporary Australia*, ed. Lynette Russell (Honolulu: Hawai'i University Press, 2003), 43–65.

Sonia Maria Melchiorre, 'Winterson's Adaptations for the Stage and the Screen', *Jeanette Winterson*, ed. Sonya Andermahr (London and New York: Continuum, 2007), 130–145.

Nicola M. Merola, 'Materializing a Geotraumatic and Melancholy Anthropocene: Jeanette Winterson's *The Stone Gods*', *Minnesota Review* 83 (2014): 91–112.

Jurgen Moltmann, *God in Creation: A New Theology of Creation and the Spirit of God*, trans. Margaret Kohl (Minneapolis: Fortress, 1993).

Jason W. Moore, *Capitalism in the Web of Life: Ecology and the Accumulation of Capital* (New York: Verso, 2015).

Timothy Morton, 'Ecology Without the Present', *Oxford Literary Review* 34.2 (2012): 229–238.

Viviane K. Namaste, *Invisible Lives: The Erasure of Transsexual and Transgendered People* (Chicago and London: Chicago University Press, 2000).

Susana Onega, *Jeanette Winterson* (Manchester: Manchester University Press, 2006).

Susana Onega, 'The Trauma Paradigm and the Ethics of Affect in Jeanette Winterson's *The Stone Gods*', *Ethics and Trauma in Contemporary British Fiction*, ed. Susana Onega and Jean-Michel Ganteau (Amsterdam: Rodopi, 2011), 265–298.

Rudolph Otto, *The Idea of the Holy: An Inquiry into the Non-rational Factor in the Idea of the Divine and its Relation to the Rational* (London: Oxford University Press, 1923).

Elaine Pagels, *Adam, Eve, and the Serpent* (New York: Vintage, 1989).

Paulina Palmer, 'The Passion: Storytelling, Fantasy, Desire', *'I'm Telling You Stories': Jeanette Winterson and the Politics of Reading*, ed. Helena Grice and Tim Woods (Amsterdam: Rodopi, 1998), 103–116.

Judith Plaskow, *Standing Again on Sinai: Judaism from a Feminist Perspective* (San Francisco: Harper & Row, 1990).

Maria Popova, 'Jeanette Winterson on Time, Language, Reading and How Art Creates a Sanctified Space for the Human Spirit', *Brain Pickings* (2014), https://www.brainpickings.org/2014/07/21/jeanette-winterson-elinor-wachtel-interview.

Jeffrey Roessner, 'Writing a History of Difference: Jeanette Winterson's "Sexing the Cherry" and Angela Carter's "Wise Children"', *College Literature* 29.1 (2002): 102–122.

Eve Kosofsky Sedgwick, *Epistemology of the Closet* (Berkeley: University of California Press, 2008).

Gershom Sholem, *Major Trends in Jewish Mysticism* (New York: Schocken, 1995).

Elaine Showalter, 'Eternal Triangles: Jeanette Winterson's *The PowerBook* is Lost in Space', *Guardian* (2000), https://www.theguardian.com/books/2000/sep/02/fiction.jeanettewinterson1.

Susan Stewart, *On Longing: Narratives of the Miniature, the Gigantic, the Souvenir, the Collection* (Durham and London: Duke University Press, 1993).

Darko Suvin, *Metamorphoses of Science Fiction* (New Haven and London: Yale University Press, 1979).

Mark C. Taylor, *Erring: A Postmodern A/theology* (Chicago and London: University of Chicago Press, 1984).

Mark C. Taylor, *About Religion: Economies of Faith in Virtual Culture* (Chicago: University of Chicago Press, 1999).

Paul Tillich, *Theology of Culture*, ed. Robert Kimball (London, Oxford and New York: Oxford University Press, 1959).

Alan Unterman, ed., *The Kabbalistic Tradition*, trans. Alan Unterman (London: Penguin, 2008).

Gianni Vattimo, *Belief*, trans. Luca D'Isanto (Stanford: Stanford University Press, 1999).

Uri Wernik, 'Will the Real Homosexual in the Bible Please Stand Up?', *Theology & Sexuality* 11.3 (2005): 47–64.

Terry R. Wright, *The Genesis of Fiction: Modern Novelists as Biblical Interpreters* (London: Ashgate, 2007).

Slavoj Žižek, *The Year of Living Dangerously* (New York: Verso, 2012).

Index

Ahmed, Sara 28, 95, 167, 176, 189, 199
Althaus-Reid 2, 18, 29, 69, 70, 75, 76, 174, 176, 184, 185
Apocalypse 149–161
Andermahr, Sonya 40, 52, 62, 63, 100, 121, 122, 141, 173, 179, 182, 189, 193, 196
Art & Lies 2, 6, 11, 15, 33, 71, 87–102, 106, 115, 122, 127, 133, 138, 165
Art Objects 5, 6, 56, 58, 98, 165
Augustine 20, 39, 40, 41, 65, 178

Badiou, Alain 2, 46, 47, 48, 53, 54, 58, 91, 157, 168, 180, 181, 182, 198, 200
Bahktin, Mikhail 62
Barthes, Roland 51, 122, 180
Baudrillard, Jean 120, 123, 130, 192
Bauman, Zygmunt 56, 181
bisexuality 1, 6, 10, 11, 29, 45, 57, 81, 82, 83, 103
Boating for Beginners 1, 31–44, 116, 127, 146, 176–178
Boesel, Chris 18, 174, 185
Bradley, F. H 96
Brown, Wendy 56, 90, 181, 188
Bultmann, Rudolph 23
Butler, Judith 6, 83, 85, 93, 145, 175, 186, 187, 188, 197
Burns, Christy 11, 98, 172, 189

Caputo, John D 2, 9, 33, 34, 37, 40, 54, 55, 58, 83, 99, 128, 146, 147, 166, 168, 176, 178, 181, 182, 187, 191, 194, 197, 200
Certeau, Michel de 12, 107, 113, 114, 173, 192
climate change 149–161
Cohen, Jeffrey Jerome 61, 182

Crary, Jonathan 88, 89, 101, 188
Creed, Barbara 61, 182

Darwin, Charles 133, 134, 140, 141, 145, 147
deconstruction 7, 9, 105, 132, 163–165
Deleuze, Gillies 54, 83, 181
DeLillo, Don 12, 145, 146, 169, 173
Denby, Michelle 21, 53, 175, 181
Derrida, Jacques 2, 8, 9, 10, 11, 13, 14, 34, 40, 77, 78, 82, 84, 109, 114, 129, 131, 132, 166, 172, 173, 178, 185, 187, 192, 194
Doan, Laura 6
Dolezal, Luna 153, 160, 198, 199

Eckhart, Meister 75, 185
Eliade, Mircea 57, 58, 98, 145, 154, 182, 197, 198
Ellis, Havelock 20
Epicurus 97
Event 45–59

feminism 4, 6, 11, 17, 35, 62–65
feminist theology 2, 18–19, 35, 38–43, 65–71
Finney, Brian 75, 185
Foucault, Michel 20, 47, 57, 97, 174, 181, 189
Freud, Sigmund 38, 66, 127, 142, 161, 177, 184, 194, 196, 199
Frye, Northrop 7, 23, 32, 34, 42, 137, 171, 175

Game of Thrones 89
Ghosh, Amitav 149, 197
Grice, Helena and Tim Woods 62, 103, 105, 182, 190

Gustar, Jennifer 12, 172
Gut Symmetries 1, 2, 10, 15, 57, 103–117, 119, 126, 141, 142, 150, 166–167

Halberstam, Jack 80, 85, 122, 187, 188, 193
Hale, Jacob 80, 187
Halperin, David 20
Hansen, Regina 81, 82, 187
Hardt, Michael 92, 188
Harvey, David 87, 88, 89, 90, 188
Haslett, Jane 63, 183
Hayles, N. Katherine 121, 125, 193
Heschel, Abraham 22, 23, 25, 175
Hobbes, Thomas 100, 102, 167
Holland, Mary 116, 123, 172, 173, 192, 193
The Hunger Games 89

internet 119–127, 130–132

Jameson, Fredric 89, 92, 101, 151, 188
Jane Eyre 24
Johnson, Elizabeth 69, 184
Judaism 2, 15, 19, 33, 34, 36, 63, 103, 105, 106–112
Justin 20

Kearney, Richard 2, 4, 8, 9, 115, 140, 142, 143, 164, 165, 171, 173, 192, 194, 196, 199
Keller, Catherine 2, 18, 38, 39, 40, 41, 42, 77, 142, 152, 155, 159, 160, 161, 174, 177,178, 185, 196, 198, 199
Kenosis 84, 125, 126
Keulks, Gavin 123, 130, 133, 136, 145, 193, 194, 195, 197
Kirby, Alan 120, 121, 192
Kristeva, Julia 5, 41, 63, 65, 66, 69, 73, 142, 178, 183, 184, 196

Lacan, Jacques 58, 65
lesbian 1, 4, 11, 17–19, 57, 76, 81, 98, 159, 179

Levinas, Emmanuel 14, 33, 34, 48, 173
Lighthousekeeping 2, 133–147, 164, 176
Lyotard, Jean-Francois 104

Irigaray, Luce 2, 40, 41, 178

Maimonides 19, 109, 110, 191
Mann, Thomas 136
Marion, Jean-Luc 83, 84, 187
Martin, Sara 64, 183
McDonald, Myfanwy 80, 186
McClure, John 126, 145, 146, 169, 194, 197
Merleau-Ponty, Maurice 12, 13
Midrash 36
Moltmann, Jurgen 125, 126, 193
Moore, Jason 154, 198
Morton, Timothy 150, 197
Mothers 61–73
mysticism 12, 107–116, 166

Namaste, Vivian 78, 186
Negative theology 75–86, 109–110, 114, 166
neoliberalism 46, 58, 87–102, 165
Nicolas of Cusa 75, 77, 166, 185
Nietzsche, Friedrich 2, 7, 40
Noah 31–44

Onega, Susana 19, 22, 63, 64, 93, 104, 106, 115, 133, 138, 139, 140, 157, 161, 174, 175, 182, 183, 189, 190, 192, 195, 197, 198, 199
Otto, Rudolph 49, 180
Oranges Are Not the Only Fruit 1, 2, 7, 14, 15, 17–30, 37, 42, 72, 90, 131, 133, 163

Palmer, Paulina 72, 184
The Passion 1, 2, 3, 6, 13–15, 28, 45–59, 71, 91, 96, 106, 124, 129, 132, 133, 144, 152, 168
Pentecostal 15, 23, 138

Plaskow, Judith 19, 34, 35, 174, 177
The PowerBook 1, 10, 51, 57, 101, 119–132, 150, 163
postmodernism 1, 4, 5, 6, 7, 8, 12, 17, 31, 58, 62, 89, 92, 104, 105, 117, 119, 120, 123, 124, 132, 133, 134, 135, 136, 141, 144, 145, 146, 152, 153, 156, 165, 169
post-postmodernism 12, 117, 123, 165, 169
post-secular 3, 5, 8, 28, 34, 124, 146–147, 163, 169
Pseudo-Dionysius 75
prophets 22–26, 155
Pynchon, Thomas 145, 146, 169

Quantum physics 103–106
queer theology 2, 14, 27, 29, 69, 75, 77
queer theory 1, 12, 17–19

Roessner, Jeffrey 69, 71, 184

Sedgwick, Eve Kosofsky 17, 20, 82, 84, 173, 187
Seeskin, Kenneth 110
Sexing the Cherry 6, 61–73

sexuality 1, 17–21
Sholem, Gershom 108, 111, 190
Showalter, Elaine 10, 119, 172, 192
Song of Songs 42, 128
Stewart, Susan 64, 68, 183
The Stone Gods 149–161, 169
Suvin, Darko 149, 197
The Strange Case of Dr Jekyll and Mr Hyde 133, 144, 145
Strauss, Richard 87, 100

Tanglewreck 90, 188
Taylor, Mark C 3, 4, 9, 123, 124, 126, 164, 171, 172, 193, 199
Tillich, Paul 3, 4, 171
Treasure Island 133
Transgender 32, 79–80, 85, 122
Tzimtzum 110, 111, 126, 191

Woolf, Virginia 96, 115, 133
Wright, Terry 15, 37, 173, 176, 177
Written on the Body 1, 2, 6, 7, 10, 12, 13, 57, 75–86, 107, 108, 157, 166–167

Zizek, Slavoj 94, 189
The Zohar 107

www.ingramcontent.com/pod-product-compliance
Lightning Source LLC
Chambersburg PA
CBHW052040300426
44117CB00012B/1909